A GUIDE

TO THE

TEXTUAL CRITICISM

OF THE

NEW TESTAMENT.

BY EDWARD MILLER, M.A.

RECTOR OF BUCKNELL, OXON.

Οἱ λόγοι Μου οὐ μὴ παρέλθωσι.—ST. MATT. xxiv. 35.
"Truth crushed to earth shall rise again."—BRYANT.

DEAN BURGON SOCIETY PRESS
Box 354
Collingswood, New Jersey 08108
Website: www.DeanBurgonSociety.org
ISBN 1-888328-09-6

Published by
The Dean Burgon Society Press
Box 354
Collingswood, New Jersey 08108
U.S.A.
Web: DeanBurgonSociety.org
Phone: 856-854-4452

Original edition: 1886
Reprinted: July, 1979
Hardback edition: July, 2003

Copyright, 2003
All Rights Reserved

ISBN #1-888328-09-6

Foreword

Introduction to the 1979 Reprint

THE DEAN BURGON SOCIETY, INCORPORATED [Box 354, Collingswood, New Jersey 08108] gives great praise to God for His blessings upon our organization which began November, 1978, in Philadelphia, Pennsylvania.

Object #9 of the DEAN BURGON SOCIETY is "*To acquire, print, sell, and distribute other sound books by the scholars who lived around the time of Dean John William Burgon who defended the Traditional Masoretic Hebrew Text, the Traditional Received Greek Text, and the King James Version,...*" [*DEAN BURGON NEWS,* January, 1979, p. 4 (subscription available for a GIFT to DBS of $3.50 per year; $7.00 per year for Foreign and Canadian subscribers)].

This present REPRINT of *A GUIDE TO THE TEXTUAL CRITICISM OF THE NEW TESTAMENT* by Edward Miller is the Society's FIRST in a series, hopefully, of books which further its purposes **"IN DEFENSE OF TRADITIONAL BIBLE TEXTS,"** as the Lord raises up the funds and supplies our needs.

The significance of this present volume by Miller lies in the fact that Edward Miller was Dean John William Burgon's understudy and co-worker. He published at least two of Burgon's works posthumously *(The Traditional Text of the Holy Gospels*--**#1159**, and *Causes of Corruptions of the Traditional Text*--**#1160**) and coupled his own personal talents and ability for this textual work with the close personal training from Burgon, the master, himself.

This book is brief and yet profoundly needed to offset the unfounded and unscriptural books on textual criticism which have been based upon the faulty and false Westcott and Hort Greek textual theories in whole or in part. We hope and pray that a copy of it might find its way into every library of every college, university, Bible Institute, seminary, and other school of higher learning; into every library of every Pastor in the country; into every library of every church in the country; and into the hands of every scholar and layman alike whose sincere and genuine desire is to ascertain, amidst the false beacon-lights which have been especially shining since 1881, the solid and proper principles on which to determine the exact words of the New Testament Scriptures.

For other books in this **REPRINT SERIES** as they come out, see the **ORDER PAGES** in the back of this book or write THE DEAN BURGON SOCIETY, Box 354, Collingswood, New Jersey 08108. Pastor D. A. Waite (Th.D., Ph.D.) President, THE DEAN BURGON SOCIETY

Sincerely for God's Written Words,

D. A. Waite

DAW/w   Pastor D. A. Waite, Th.D., Ph.D.
President, THE DEAN BURGON SOCIETY

The Dean Burgon Society
In Defense of Traditional Bible Texts
Box 354
Collingswood, NJ 08108, U.S.A.

TO THOSE

WHO,

WHETHER AT THE OUTSET OF THE WORK, OR AT THE CLOSE,

HAVE KINDLY GIVEN HELP OR ENCOURAGEMENT,

This little Treatise

IS GRATEFULLY INSCRIBED,

WITH THE PRAYER,

THAT IT MAY MINISTER IN SOME DEGREE, HOWEVER HUMBLE,

TO THE ASCERTAINMENT AND ACCEPTANCE

OF

THE GENUINE WORDS OF HOLY SCRIPTURE.

ERRATA.

Page 2, line 20, *read* xxiv. 51 *for* xxiv. 15.
Page 3, line 9, *read* the *for* its.
Page 7, line 2, *read* affected *for* effected.
Page 9, line 20, *read* manuscript *for* manuscripts.
Page 13, line 21, *read* appeared *for* apeared.
Page 17, line 17, *read* 5 *for* 4.
Page 21, line 14, *read* manuscripts *for* manuscript.
Page 27, line 4, *read* Arian *for* Asian.
Page 54, note 3, *read* ix. 14 *for* ii. 14.
Page 56, note 2, *read* collating *for* collecting.
Page 73, line 23, *read* The *for* That.
Page 93, note, *read* contravened *for* controvened.
Page 95, line 6, *read* Lucar *for* Lucas.
Page 112, note 3, *read* 3 *for* 4.
Page 121, line 20, *read* Itacism *for* Italicism.
Page 128, line 23, *read* authenticity *for* authencity.

PREFACE.

THE ensuing treatise is intended to be a brief Manual on the Textual Criticism of the New Testament for ordinary students of the Bible, and to induce those who may be disposed to enter more deeply into the important subject of it to prosecute further research in "The Plain Introduction" of Dr. Scrivener, the learned works of Dean Burgon, and in other well-known sources of information upon Textual Criticism.

The foot-notes will ordinarily indicate how much I have been indebted to the labours of other men in a work which pretends to be little more than a faithful representation of stores accumulated by the learned, and an independent estimate of the conclusions drawn by them.

To the Dean of Chichester I am indebted for many previous hints which I have found invaluable during my prosecution of a task both laborious and difficult. The undertaking of it was originally pressed upon me from without, and I am myself convinced that some such assistance as is here offered to the general Reader is greatly needed at this time. But I lay down my pen with the conviction derived from the accomplishment of my work, that every Reader who would really understand, and form an opinion for himself upon the great questions at stake, must bestow on the problem which has suddenly emerged into prominence a considerable amount of individual, unprejudiced attention. He will be able to see with which of the contending parties the Truth must lie : but he must approach the problem in a calm, judicial spirit, must require Proof (as far as Proof is attainable) instead of putting up with Hypothesis, and above all must never cease to exercise a large amount of vigilant sagacity,—in fact, of Common Sense.

My thanks are also due to the Rev. R. Hutchison, M.A., Rector of Woodeaton, and late Scholar of Exeter College, Oxford, who has kindly helped me in correcting the proof sheets.

E. M.

BUCKNELL RECTORY,
    Ember Week, Sept., 1885.

CONTENTS.

CHAPTER I.

INTRODUCTION. IMPORTANCE OF THE SUBJECT.

The question stated—seven instances of serious change—others also advocated—the number introduced into the Revised Version—more into other editions—the subject not generally known—importance of it —plan of the work . . . . pp. 1-5.

CHAPTER II.

HISTORY OF TEXTUAL CRITICISM.

FIRST PART. EARLIER STAGES.

The natural growth of the science influenced by investigation and discovery . . . . pp. 6-7.

I. Infancy :—The New Testament not printed till the sixteenth century—1. Complutensian Polyglott. 2. Erasmus. 3. Robert Stephen, Theodore Beza, and the Elzevirs—the Received Text . pp. 7-12.

II. Childhood :—Introduction of various readings. 1. Bishop Walton, Codex A, Courcelles, and Fell. 2. Mill. 3. Bentley, Codex B. 4. Bengel, Wetstein, Matthæi, Birch, Alter, and Moldenhawer. 5. Griesbach, families and recensions of manuscripts, and Scholz— the free advance of boyhood . . . . . . pp. 12-19.

CHAPTER III.

HISTORY OF TEXTUAL CRITICISM (*continued*).

SECOND PART. CONTEMPORARY GROWTH . p. 20.

III. Youth :—Impatience under an overwhelming mass of materials—

Extreme Textualism. 1. Lachmann—rejects all but a few witnesses. 2. Tregelles—follows Lachmann—great services in collating and editing. 3. Tischendorf—amazing labours—discovers the Sinaitic—zigzag course. 4. Drs. Westcott and Hort—develop Lachmann's principles—extreme deference to B—surprising results—followed mainly by Two Members of the Revisers' Company—must we follow them? pp. 20-30.

IV. Signs of Coming Maturity :—Opposition. 1. Dr. Scrivener—his published works—large-minded principles. 2. Dean Burgon—his works—misrepresented—his sound and wide principles. 3. Canon Cook—The Bishops Wordsworth, J. G. Reiche, Kuenen and Cobet, Dr. Michelsen, Vercellone, Ceriani, Abbè Martin—other Roman Catholics . . . . pp. 30-37.

CHAPTER IV.

SCHOOL OF EXTREME TEXTUALISM.

The origin attributed by the leading masters to Lachmann . p. 38

A. Theory of Drs. Westcott and Hort. 1. Knowledge of Documents derived from date and character a prior requisite : B and ℵ are the best MSS. 2. Importance of Genealogy, under which these two MSS. are brought back nearly to the Apostolic autographs. 3. Four families, sc. (*a*) Syrian, made in a recension at Antioch, (*b*) Western, (*c*) Alexandrian, and (*d*) Neutral, which is the best. 4. Of these, two are corrupt (*b* and *c*); the Neutral alone reaches back to earliest times; Syrian shewn to be worthless by analysis, want of antiquity, and internal evidence. 5. Hence ℵ B together nearly always right, and B alone seldom wrong . . . . pp. 38-44.

B. Refutation. 1. Too easy to be true, grounded on only part of the evidence, and destitute of real proof. 2. Sound sense is violated, and opinion unsupported by facts is balanced by opinions of other masters. 3. Genealogy affords an unsafe analogy, and in fact points the opposite way. B and ℵ are also condemned for want of descendants. 4. The theory about Families is disallowed by other Doctors, and lacks evidence. 5. The "Syrian," or Traditional Text, is not proved to be posterior, whether by an imaginary recension, or by a fanciful theory of conflation, or by ignoring proof of early existence, or by supposed internal evidence. 6. The characters of B and ℵ not superfine;

they were rejected by the Church, were the products of Semiarian times, are condemned by experts, and are full of blunders . pp. 44-59

CHAPTER V.

THE RIVAL SCHOOL.

The tenets of the Rival School already implied—1. They do not maintain the Received Text, and are not indiscriminate in the use of authorities. 2. Insist that all authorities should be weighed and employed ; and thus widen the basis. 3. They maintain the Traditional Text, which the Church of all ages has acknowledged, and no age therefore can reject—extreme importance of this part of the contention ; hence the need of a history of the Traditional Text—the question depends upon a just estimate of proportion . . . pp. 60-64.

CHAPTER VI.

HISTORY OF THE TRADITIONAL TEXT TILL THE ERA OF ST. CHRYSOSTOM.

Difference between Sacred and Classical Textual Criticism. 1. Conjectural Emendation inadmissible. 2. God the Holy Ghost the Preserver as well as Inspirer of the Holy Scriptures. 3. Corporate as well as individual productions . . . . . pp. 65-68.

Early Corruption derived from oral teaching, tampering with the text by heretics, carelessness of scribes, ignorance of Greek or of doctrine—Gnosticism—Marcion—Tatian—evidence of corruption . pp. 68-72.

Exceeding care employed by the faithful—Traditional Text—Peshito —Old Latin Versions—Egyptian . . . . . pp. 72-77.

Alexandria—Origen—followers of Origen—Eusebius—persecution of Diocletian—celebrated order of Constantine—transcription of B and ℵ
pp. 77-83.

Proofs of the Traditional Text in this period found amidst corruption in its subsequent supremacy, in the MSS. used by the Fathers, and in contemporaneous Versions . . . . . . pp. 83-85.

CHAPTER VII.

HISTORY OF THE TRADITIONAL TEXT FROM THE ERA OF ST. CHRYSOSTOM TILL THE INVENTION OF PRINTING.

The previous period an era of speculation—the great Patristic Era—commentaries, dictionaries, and grammars—punctuation—breathings—spelling — improvement in the art of Transcription — monasteries — ibraries—canon of Holy Scripture—supremacy of the Traditional Text
pp. 86-94.

Gothic Version—Codex Alexandrinus (A)—Parisian Codex (C)—the Fathers not uncritical—Uncial manuscripts—Versions—Vulgate—Armenian—Georgian—Ethiopian—other Uncials . pp. 94-100.

Cursive manuscripts—their value—their agreement with the Uncials—Lectionaries—other Versions—undisputed predominance of the Traditional Text . . . . pp. 100-104.

CHAPTER VIII.

MATERIALS OF CRITICISM.

I. (a) Uncial manuscripts—in Gospels, Acts and Catholic Epistles, Pauline Epistles, and Apocalypse . . . . pp. 105-106.

(b) Cursive manuscripts—their value and vast number pp. 106-107.

Table of Uncials . . . . pp. 108-109.

II. Lectionaries and Liturgies—lectionary-system—their value—influence in mischief—Evangelistaria—Praxapostoli—Liturgies
pp. 110-112.

III. Versions—Table—value—drawbacks—Old Latin pp. 113-115.

IV. Ecclesiastical Writers—drawbacks—value—the oldest class of manuscripts, but at second hand . . . . pp. 116-117.

The field to be explored—MSS. at first hand wanting in antiquity
p. 117.

CHAPTER IX.

PRINCIPLES OF CRITICISM.

No evidence must be discarded—responsibility of the Church—

1. The first object the discovery of the Traditional Text—begin with the Received Text. 2. All evidence must be mastered—and followed. 3. Internal Evidence not on a par with External proof—seven canons—conclusion . . . . pp. 118-122.

APPENDIX I. The last Twelve Verses of St. Mark's Gospel
pp. 125-127.
,, II. The First Word from the Cross . pp. 127-128.
,, III. The Record of the strengthening Angel, the Agony, and the Bloody Sweat . . pp. 128-130.
,, IV. The Angelic Hymn . . . pp. 130-131.
,, V. The Doxology in the Lord's Prayer pp. 131-133.
,, VI. The Son of GOD's Eternal Existence in Heaven
pp. 133-134.
,, VII. GOD manifested in The Flesh . pp. 134-137.

A GUIDE TO THE TEXTUAL CRITICISM OF THE NEW TESTAMENT.

CHAPTER I.

INTRODUCTION.

IMPORTANCE OF THE SUBJECT.

WHAT is the genuine Greek—what the true Text of the New Testament? Which are the very words which were written by the Evangelists and Apostles of our Lord Jesus Christ under the Inspiration of the Holy Ghost? Have we up to this period received and used for the information of our faith and the guidance of our lives a Form of Text, which in a vast number of particulars, many of which are of great importance, has been fabricated by the device or error of men?

This question has been raised in the research of recent times, which has brought to light an amount of evidence residing in ancient copies and translations of the New Testament, that has led many eminent scholars to reject, as being in their estimation corruptions of the pure Text, various passages which have endeared themselves to Christians in the course of centuries. Thus, according to principles largely adopted,

(a) The Last Twelve Verses of the Gospel according to

St. Mark must be cast aside, and an abrupt close made after the words, 'for they were afraid.'

(b) In the Lord's Prayer as given by St. Luke (xi. 2-4), the following clauses must be excised:—'Our .... which art in Heaven'; 'Thy will be done, as in Heaven, so on earth';—' but deliver us from evil.'

(c) The Doxology must be omitted from the Lord's Prayer in St. Matthew (vi. 13), and so all record of it lost in the Gospels.

(d) Vv. 43, 44 must no longer be reckoned in the 22nd chapter of St. Luke, and thereby the account must disappear of the strengthening Angel and the 'Bloody Sweat,' as well as the evangelical record of 'the Agony in the Garden.'

(e) The first of our Lord's seven Sayings from the Cross (St. Luke xxiii. 34) must be regarded as unauthentic, 'Father, forgive them, for they knew not what they do.'

(f) Also St. Luke's assertion of the Ascent into Heaven (xxiv. 15),—an omission of the more importance, because St. Mark's account of the same event, which included also the session at the Right Hand of GOD, is supposed under these principles to have vanished with the last twelve verses of his Gospel.

(g) St. Luke's recital of the Institution of the Holy Sacrament (xxii. 19, 20) must be lost, except as far as 'This is My Body.'

These seven instances, which might be multiplied extensively by the addition of other omissions,—such as of the descending angel and the cure wrought in the pool of Bethesda, of the last cry in St. Mark's description of the centurion's faith, of the greater part of St. Luke's account of the Inscription on the Cross, of St. Peter's visit to the Sepulchre in the same Gospel, of the salutation 'Peace be unto you,' of the Lord shewing His Hands and His Feet, of the word 'broken,' whereby a gash is made and a blank space left in St. Paul's grand version of the Institution of the Holy Sacrament, and others too numerous to recount here —not to do more than allude to startling statements, such as that our Lord's Side was pierced before death, and that the sun was eclipsed at its full,[1]—may teach all who revere and love the Word of God what precious points are at stake. If the changes advocated by the modern school leave enough behind in Holy Writ to support without doubt the essentials of the Faith of Christendom, yet they are so momentous in themselves as to produce a painful wrench in earnest affections which have attached themselves to words familiar and deeply loved from childhood, and to prove that, at least to first appearance, general and special attention should be directed to what may really be a corruption of the Holy Scriptures. Besides this, the number of alterations, amounting in the most moderate of the new recensions to 5,337,[2] reveals the formidable nature of the operations that are threatened. If the majority of these alterations are small, it must be remembered that the instance taken is one which presents much less change than other editions of the New Testa-

---

[1] St. John v. 3, 4 : St. Mark xv. 39 : St. Luke xxiii. 38 : xxiv. 12 : xxiv. 36 : xxiv. 40 : 1 Cor. ix. 24, κλώμενον : St. Matt. xxvii. 49 : St. Luke xxiii. 45. ἐκλείποντος, which, as Dean Burgon truly says ("Revision Revised," p. 65), 'means an eclipse of the sun and no other thing,' though the Revisers translate it 'the sun's light failing.'

[2] The number of changes in the Greek Text of the Revised Version as estimated by Dr. Scrivener (Burgon, "The Revision Revised," p. 405). The changes in the English of the Revised Version are said to amount to 36,191.

ment. Enough is shown to establish beyond doubt that it is the duty of all Christians, who take an intelligent interest in the controversies of their day, not to sit still when such concerns are in jeopardy.

Yet at the present time there are comparatively few persons, clerical or lay, who have an intelligent acquaintance with the grounds on which this important question rests. The subject at first sight presents a forbidding aspect to most minds:—the exceedingly valuable treatises on it are too full of learning, and too long for such as are not really students to master:—and the hurry and haste of modern life demand a simpler mode of treatment.

It is therefore with the hope of presenting the chief features of Textual Criticism, or such elementary considerations as are immediately involved in determining the Greek Text of the New Testament, to readers in a clear and not uninteresting way, that in deference to the urgent solicitations of some who enter deeply into the controversy, the composition of this little treatise has been undertaken. Inexpressibly dear to all true Christians, whether they range themselves on the one side or the other, must be the very expressions,—the sentences, the phrases, the words, and even the rhythm and the accents,—of the genuine utterance of the Holy Spirit of GOD. The general sentiment of Christianity has applied with plenary enlargement the warning given at the close of the last Book in the Bible against addition or omission.[1] 'Let no man add to the words of the Holy Scriptures or detract anything from them,' said one of the most renowned of the Fathers.[2] 'Let

---

[1] Rev. xxii. 18, 19.
[2] Athanasius, "Ex Festali Epistola," xxxix. (t. ii. p. 39, Ed. Colon).

them fear the woe which is destined for them who add to or take away,' was the consentient admonition of another.[1]

The leading points in the contention on either side will be given in the Narrative. The questions in debate are questions of fact, and must be decided by the facts of history, the origin and nature of the documents on which they depend, and due regard to the proportion of the Christian Faith. They cannot be settled piecemeal. All the counts of the case must be before the court. An attempt will therefore be now made to represent with all candour the chief grounds on which opinion should rest, as they have been set forth in the career of the Science of Textual Criticism, in the principal arguments employed by the Rival Schools of the present day, in the history of the transmission of the New Testament from age to age, and in the leading Materials of Criticism; and it will be our duty to deduce in conclusion the main principles that ought to regulate critical operations in any endeavour to revise and remodel the Sacred Text.

[1] Tertullian, "Adv. Hermogenem," xxii.

CHAPTER II.

HISTORY OF TEXTUAL CRITICISM.

FIRST PART. EARLIER STAGES. (1) INFANCY :—FORMATION OF THE 'RECEIVED TEXT.' (2) CHILDHOOD :— CRITICAL OPERATIONS BEFORE 1830.

THE Science of sacred Textual Criticism is the child of circumstances, and has been fostered by the zeal and industry of learned men. It has arisen from the large number of existing Copies of the New Testament, which has now, so far as inquiry has extended, reached no less than some two thousand.[1] These primary sources of information are further augmented by Translations into various languages, and by quotations occurring in the works of early Ecclesiastical Writers. Accordingly, as these numerous witnesses render evidence which is discordant in thousands of particulars, there is plainly a need of guiding principles and of a recognised system in estimating their testimony. Thus the Science of sacred Textual Criticism has been gradually growing almost since the time of the invention of printing.

And as was natural, its growth and tendency have been largely influenced from time to time by the materials that research and discovery have continually produced. When new Manuscripts have been brought to light, or the verdict of old ones has been ascertained by the slow process of col-

---

[1] 2003. Burgon, "The Revision Revised," p. 521. Dean Burgon added 374 in 1883. Dr. Scrivener, including these 374, reckons 2094. "Plain Introduction," Appendix, p. xxx, 3rd edition.

lation, the importation of fresh evidence has necessarily effected the conclusions previously drawn. A science depending upon facts that can be ascertained only after protracted processes of investigation, cannot but be late in coming to maturity. At the present time, hundreds of Manuscripts are waiting to be collated, various Versions need re-editing, and indexes have to be provided of the quotations in the Fathers, before all that is to be said upon controverted points can be collected with exact accuracy. Besides that, the relative value of the various classes and subdivisions of evidence cannot yet be determined so as to meet with universal acceptance.

Four Periods in the history of Textual Criticism may be distinguished, so far as it has been yet evolved, viz., Infancy, Childhood, Impetuous Youth, and Incipient Maturity.

I. THE INFANCY.

Although a folio edition of the Bible in Latin was printed by Gutenberg as early as A.D. 1455, none in the original Greek appeared till the beginning of the sixteenth century. The demand at the time was not great. Greek Scribes dependent upon employment for their living abounded in Europe after the capture of Constantinople in 1453. Printing would be much more difficult in the unfamiliar Greek type: and the prevalence of clever and graceful abbreviations made the work of copying at once more rapid and more artistic. Therefore half a century passed by before the Church saw the accomplishment of a task so formidable, of which the want was at once so easily and so well supplied.

1. Cardinal Ximenes, founder of the University of Alcalà, and an eminent patron of literature, was first in the field. In

the course of his advancement he had passed from a dungeon, where he had spent six years of his life, to the Archbishopric of Toledo and the Regency of Castile; and in his later days laid out the vast income of his See upon charitable or public objects. Having collected together as many Manuscripts as he could, he set Lopez de Stunica and other learned editors to the work in 1502, on which he expended more than 50,000 ducats, or about £23,000. It was intended to commemorate the birth of Charles V. But many years elapsed ere the completion of the New Testament in Greek and Latin on Jan. 10, 1514; and the book was not published till 1520, after Ximenes' death, and did not get into general circulation till two years after.

The Complutensian Polyglott—for such was the title, derived from the Latin name (*Complutum*) of Alcalà—was said by the editors to have been constructed from selected Manuscripts of great age and accuracy, supplied by Pope Leo X., who was the patron of the undertaking. Attempts have been made without success to ascertain what these Manuscripts were. The only result is that we must abide by the assertion of the editors and the character of the work. The Complutensian is admitted to be a fair but not by any means a faultless edition of the text that had already been in vogue, as is universally admitted, for upwards of a thousand years.

2. But the Complutensian Polyglott was actually anticipated in publication by a Greek Testament in Germany.

Froben, the printer of Basle, hearing of the operations in Spain, and wishing to forestall them, sent to Erasmus, who was then staying in England, and pressed him earnestly to undertake the office of editor. Erasmus received the first overtures on April 17, 1515. But such was the haste made that the New Testament was printed before the end of February, 1516. Erasmus had however, as it appears, made some preparations of his own before he heard from Froben. He seems to have used what copies he could procure, but in a few cases where he either found or supposed his Greek authorities to be deficient, he translated from the Vulgate into Greek.[1]

Erasmus' first edition made its way into Spain, where the Complutensian was lying complete, but awaiting the Pope's imprimatur for publication. Stunica found fault with it in the spirit of rivalry: but the fine old Cardinal replied, 'Would that all the Lord's people were prophets! produce better if thou canst; condemn not the industry of another.'[2]

Erasmus was, however, attacked by Stunica, and also by Edward Lee, afterward Archbishop of York, because he had omitted the testimony of the heavenly Witnesses in 1 John v. 7, as well as on other grounds. Erasmus replied that he could not find the passage in his Greek manuscripts, and that even some Latin copies did not give it. But at length he promised that if any Greek manuscripts were produced containing the words, he would in future insert them. It is remarkable that the celebrated Vatican Codex (B) was on this occasion for the first time appealed to on a point of textual criticism.[3] In course of time the Codex Montfortianus, now at Dublin, was brought forward, and in consequence the passage was printed by Erasmus in his third edition in 1522. A fourth edition exhibited the text in three parallel columns, the Greek, the Latin Vulgate, and a recension of the latter by Erasmus. The last in 1535 contained

---

[1] This was notably the case in the last six verses of the Revelation.
[2] Scrivener's "Plain Introduction," p. 431.
[3] Tregelles, "Printed Text," p. 22.

only the Greek. Each successive edition underwent correction, but the last did not differ much from the fourth. Erasmus died at Basle in 1536.

3. The editions of Robert Stephen, Theodore Beza, and the Elzevirs, complete this period.

The two first of Stephen, published at Paris respectively in 1546 and 1549, were most elegantly printed with type cast at the expense of Francis I., and are known to connoisseurs by the title 'O mirificam' from the opening words expressing an encomium upon that king's liberality. The third, in folio, came out in 1550, and for the first time in the history of editions of the Greek Testament contained various readings. Reference was made to sixteen authorities, viz., the Complutensian Polyglott and fifteen manuscripts, amongst which the Codex Bezæ (D), now at Cambridge, is thought to have been numbered.[1] Erasmus is not mentioned, although Stephen's two earliest editions were mainly grounded upon Erasmus' readings; and his third, according to Dr. Scrivener's computation, differs from them conjointly in only 361 places.[2] Robert Stephen did not collate his authorities himself, but employed the services of his son Henry.

His record of readings in the margin of his folio caused great offence to the doctors of the Sorbonne, and Stephen withdrew to Geneva to escape their enmity. Here he published in 1551 his fourth edition, almost unchanged in the Greek text from the previous one, but with one remarkable alteration. The chapters, into which Cardinal Hugo, of Santo Caro, had divided the books of the Bible in the thirteenth century, were in this edition first subdivided into

---

[1] Scrivener, "Plain Introduction," pp. 121, 438.
[2] "Plain Introduction," p. 436; i.e., 334 times in the text, and 27 in punctuation.

verses. His son Henry said that his father made the subdivision 'whilst riding' from Paris to Lyons, probably during the intervals of his exercise. His object was to facilitate reference in a Concordance which he had in prospect.[1]

Beza's text did not differ much from Stephen's. He published five editions, slightly varying upon one another, and ranging from 1565 to 1598. Of these the fourth, published in 1589, has the highest reputation, the fifth having been produced in 'extreme old age.' Besides the advantage of Stephen's collections, Beza was the possessor of two very important MSS., the one already mentioned (D of the Gospels and Acts), which was presented by him to the University of Cambridge, and the Codex Claromontanus (D of St. Paul's Epistles) at Paris, both of which contained Greek and Latin texts, being therefore 'bilingual' manuscripts.

The Elzevirs—Bonaventure and Abraham—brought out two editions at their celebrated press, one in 1624, and the other in 1633. Their text was made up from those of Stephen and Beza. The latter edition was remarkable from the expression 'Received Text' occurring for the first time. Addressing the reader they said, 'So you have now a text universally received, in which we give no alteration or corruption.'[2]

The text of Stephen, which was afterwards carefully repro-

---

[1] This is the ordinary account. Dr. Gregory however ("Prolegomena," pp. 164-66) maintains that Stephen Langton was the author of the present division into Chapters, as usual in the West. Some sort of division had been in existence from the first (Ibid. pp. 140-163).

[2] 'Textum ergo habes nunc ab omnibus receptum, in quo nihil immutatum aut corruptum damus,' referring to the edition of 1624. (Pref.)

duced by Mill, has been generally taken in England as the standard or 'Received' text, and that of the Elzevirs has been thus regarded on the continent. The translators, however, of our Authorized Version did not adhere exclusively to any one of the chief editions.[1] When their authorities were at variance, they sometimes in their interpretation of the 'Received Text' followed Beza, sometimes Stephen, sometimes the Complutensians, Erasmus, or the Latin Vulgate.

II. THE CHILDHOOD.

In the period hitherto indicated, there was hardly any weighing of opposed readings. Such as presented themselves were ordinarily accepted with implicit confidence. The free instincts of infancy guided the Science mainly along a track that had previously been trodden with the continued approval of the Church for centuries. It would be reckless haste, not discerning judgment, that would off-hand condemn results thus reached. The copies chiefly followed were known to be specimens more or less exact of what had been preserved in the Church as the recognised form of the inspired Word.[2]

The Received Text of the sixteenth and seventeenth

---

[1] Dr. Scrivener has collected 252 passages, out of which the translators follow Beza against Stephen in 113, Stephen against Beza in 59, the Complutensian, Erasmus, or the Vulgate against both Stephen and Beza in 80.—"The Authorized Edition of the English Bible," &c., by F. H. A. Scrivener, M.A., D.C.L., LL.D., Cambridge, 1884, Appendix E.

[2] This is acknowledged by both the Rival Schools of the present day. See Westcott and Hort, "Introduction," pp. 91, 92, 110, 142, 145, 146. Vol. i., pp. 547, 550, 551. Burgon, "The Revision Revised," pp. 257, 258.

centuries represented with general, but far from invariable accuracy, the Traditional Text of the previous ages of the Church. But, on the other hand, the Church of later times could not properly rest without ascertaining, by all such wide and deep inquiry as was possible, whether these instinctive processes had issued in well-grounded conclusions. What was right would be proved to be right in full and free investigation, if candour and largeness of mind and firmness in faith kept away prejudice and narrowness and unbelief.

1. In 1657, Brian Walton, afterwards Bishop of Chester, published a Polyglott, to which were appended some various readings both in the fifth and sixth volumes. In company with some colleagues he had devoted himself to this work for twelve years during the dark troubles that had befallen the Church of England. He included various readings from the Codex Alexandrinus (A), now in the British Museum, which had been presented by Cyril Lucar to Charles I. in 1628. There were comprised in his pages also the results of collations of sixteen Manuscripts made by Archbishop Ussher.

In the next year apeared at Amsterdam a New Testament by Curcellæus or Courcelles, marked by Socinian tendencies. And soon after, in 1675, Dr. John Fell, Bishop of Oxford, published a small edition, in which collations from fresh Manuscripts were given, and citations were added from the Memphitic or ancient Version of Lower Egypt, and the Gothic, which was made soon after the Goths settled on the confines of the Roman Empire.

2. But a greater and stronger start was made at the end of the seventeenth century. In large measure through the help of Bishop Fell, who during his lifetime supplied impetus and funds, Dr. John Mill devoted the labour of

thirty years to the preparation of a grand New Testament which was intended to surpass Stephen's in beauty as well as in other respects. The good bishop's death in 1686 seems to have delayed the work: and it was not till 1707, three years after Archbishop Sharpe obtained for the struggling editor a stall at Canterbury and Royal aid in the prosecution of his purpose, that the volume came out. Mill himself died just a fortnight after the publication. Thenceforward the science of Textual Criticism proceeded upon a new career.

Mill only attempted to reproduce the text of Stephen, though he has departed from it in a few particulars.[1] But he added some 30,000 readings, and an invaluable Prolegomena. He far excelled all his contemporaries and predecessors in accuracy of collation and comprehensiveness of method. "Of the criticism of the New Testament in the hands of Dr. John Mill it may be said, that he found the edifice of wood, and left it marble."[2]

3. We now come to the grand design of the great Richard Bentley, Master of Trinity College, Cambridge, which broke forth with lofty promise but never reached realization. He unfolded his plan to Archbishop Wake in a long letter, in which after explaining his own studies he professes his belief that he should be able to restore the Text of the New Testament to the form in which it was couched at the time of the Council of Nicæa. He was led in his enthusiasm to add, 'so that there shall not be twenty words, or even particles, difference.' After describing the history of the Vulgate, and the editorial labours since the invention of printing,

---

[1] Dr. Scrivener, "Plain Introduction," p. 450 and note, has specified instances of this deflection.

[2] Scrivener, "Plain Introduction," p. 448.

he concludes : ' In a word, I find that by taking 2000 errors out of the Pope's Vulgate, and as many out of the Protestant Pope Stephen's, I can set out an edition of each in columns, without using any book under 900 years old, that shall so exactly agree word for word, and, what at first amazed me, order for order, that no two tallies, nor two indentures can agree better.'[1]

This was in 1716, and in four years his plan was definitely made up. John Walker, fellow of Trinity College, who had already been employed in collating MSS. in Paris for the edition, was announced as 'overseer and corrector of the press.' John Walker continued to labour; and Bentley himself too, so far as other occupations and the strife with the Fellows of his College would allow him : but the edition never came out. He bequeathed a valuable collection of papers to his nephew, who made no use of them. After the death of the latter, they were published, including amongst several collations one which he had procured, and had got afterwards corrected, of the Vatican Manuscript (B). This was transcribed by Woide and printed.

4. A step in advance was next made by Bengel in 1734. The large number of authorities that had now come to light had created embarrassment. Were they all equally to be trusted? Did revision simply consist in a process of marshalling the witnesses on the right and left, and then counting heads? or had these witnesses special characters of their own, which must be investigated and known in order to the formation of a true estimate of their credibility?

Bengel therefore suggested that inquiries should be made into the origin of each,[1] ' whether taken singly or in pairs, or

---

[1] Ellis, "Bentleii Critica Sacra," Introductory Preface, p. xv.

associations, or families, tribes, and nations:'[1] so that they should be reduced to a genealogical table illustrating their several features and relationships. He divided manuscripts generally into African and Asiatic. In his text he was the first to depart on principle from the received standard.[2] He introduced the division of the New Testament into paragraphs, with which we have become familiar.

Bengel was followed by Wetstein, who enlarged greatly the materials ready for criticism. He spent many years in collation, including in these labours about one hundred and two Manuscripts. He was the first to cite the Manuscripts under their present designation, quoting from A to O of the Uncials in the Gospels, and 1—112 of the Cursives.[3] He attached great importance to the Codex Alexandrinus (A), the oldest then generally known. He shed much light upon the Versions, or early Translations into other languages. And he also laboured, though it is thought not so successfully, upon the Fathers. His services were so considerable that Bishop Marsh was of opinion that he had accomplished more than all his predecessors put together.[4] His edition of the Greek Testament came out in 1751-2.

Most important service was rendered in the collection and collation of existing manuscripts by C. F. Matthæi, Andrew Birch, and others. Matthæi, a Thuringian by birth, who held the Professorship of Classical Literature at Moscow, found in that capital a large number of Manuscripts brought

---

[1] Bengel, "Apparatus Criticus," p. 387.
[2] Scrivener, "Plain Introduction," p. 457.
[3] Scrivener, "Plain Introduction," p. 460. Uncial Manuscripts are those which are written in Capital Letters: Cursives, in the running hand of ordinary writing. Uncials are designated for convenience by capital letters, and Cursives by numerals.
[4] Tregelles, "Printed Text," p. 77.

in the seventeenth century from Mount Athos, both Biblical and Patristic.[1] He collated with an accuracy which has drawn down strong praise [2] seventy copies, consisting of these and some others; and besides he assembled the citations from Holy Scripture contained in about thirty manuscripts of St. Chrysostom's works. His Revision of the Greek Text was exclusively founded upon the manuscripts of his own examining. Whatever may prove to be its critical value, no difference of opinion can be entertained about the remarkable accuracy of method and scholarship, in which he has set a bright example to all who come after him. His collations will remain a treasure for all time.[2]

About the same period Alter was doing work at Vienna, similar in kind, but inferior in degree. And Birch, with the assistance of Adler and Moldenhawer, laboured in Italy, Germany, and Spain.

4. Thus a large mass of evidence grew up: what seemed vast in the days of Mill was extensively multiplied. And in consequence another attempt was made to classify the accumulated materials of criticism. John James Griesbach, a pupil of Semler, following out, though with corrections, what his master had begun, urged that three great families of manuscripts existed, each of which was founded upon a special 'Recension,' or edition. He distinguished these as respectively Western, Alexandrian, and Byzantine. He considered that the testimony of two of these classes should prevail against the third. His theory was no doubt grounded upon a certain, or rather an uncertain, amount of truth. But as he carried it out, it was overthrown by Archbishop Laurence. And as to his 'recensions,' as J. G. Reiche

---

[1] Scrivener, "Plain Introduction," p. 463.
[2] Burgon, "The Revision Revised," p. 246.

afterwards shewed,[1] there was no ground for them beyond speculation. Nothing that can be termed historical evidence has been produced for any such operations having been accomplished as would account for Griesbach's classes.

But Griesbach also carefully edited a Greek Testament, and thoroughly examined the citations of Holy Scripture made by Origen. This latter operation, of which the results may be seen in his *Symbolæ Criticæ*, affords a specimen of what must be done in the case at least of the more important Ecclesiastical Writers before all the evidence adducible can be brought to bear upon controverted points.

Griesbach carries us into the present century : he died in 1812. The work was continued by John Martin Augustine Scholz, who added, though with much incorrectness, a large amount of materials to the stores previously known. His contribution consists of no less than 616 Cursive manuscripts. But confidence cannot be reposed in his productions, as has been shewn more than once.[2] It is remarkable that he modified Griesbach's theory of supposed Recensions of manuscripts, including the Western of Griesbach amongst the Alexandrian, and thus making two instead of three. "In the Alexandrian family," says Dr. Scrivener, "he included the whole of Griesbach's Western recension, from which, indeed, it seems vain to distinguish it by any broad line of demarcation."[3]

[1] Burgon, "The Revision Revised," p. 380 and notes. Cook, "Revised Version," pp. 4-7. J. G. Reiche, "Commentarius Criticus," tom. iii., Observatio Prævia.

[2] Scrivener, "Plain Introduction," p. 474, and note, in which he quotes from Dean Burgon's letters to the "Guardian."

[3] Scrivener, "Plain Introduction," p. 475. 'The untenable point of Griesbach's system, even supposing that it had historic basis, was the impossibility of drawing an actual line of distinction between his

Such was the growth of the Science till towards the middle of the present century. It was the natural development of boyhood, invigorated and enlarged by constant action, and extending freely on all sides. There was continually an amplification of materials, and operations were progressively prosecuted over wider and wider fields. Theory was pursued less actively, and with not so happy results. Different minds succeeded in different provinces; hardly any one in all. 'We are thankful,' says Dr. Davidson, 'to the collators of manuscripts for their great labour. But it may be doubted whether they be often competent to make the best critical text out of existing materials. . . . We should rather see the collator and the editor of the text dissociated. We should like to have one person for each department.'[1]

Alexandrian and Western recensions.'—Tregelles, "Printed Text," p. 91.

[1] 'Biblical Criticism," vol. ii., pp. 104-5, quoted by Tregelles, "Printed Text," p. 172.

CHAPTER III.

HISTORY OF TEXTUAL CRITICISM.

PART II. CONTEMPORARY GROWTH. (3) YOUTH:—LACHMANN AND THE SEVERAL DOCTORS OF THE EXTREME SCHOOL. (4) SIGNS OF MATURITY:—OTHER DOCTORS. WIDENING OF THE BASIS.

BUT now came a change. The impetuosity of youth lacked the patience to await a further growth of the Science, and to abstain from drawing conclusions till all the evidence had been gathered out of all quarters, thoroughly examined, sorted, and duly valued. A short and easy method of decision was sought and taken. It was too hard a lot to leave the inheritance of the promised land to a coming generation. If the evidence were too unwieldy to be managed in the mass, some was valuable, and some not at all. Why not select the valuable, and be guided by the verdicts it gave?

So arose the School of Extreme Textualism.

1. Lachmann, the celebrated philologist and critic, published with the aid of Philip Buttmann, an edition of the New Testament in two volumes, one of which came out in 1842, and the other in 1850, and both of them at Berlin, where he was a professor. His first principle, at which he had hinted in a small edition eleven years before, was to discard

the readings of the 'Received Text,' as being in his opinion only about two centuries old; whereas they conflicted with what he conceived to be better authority. His main object was to restore, according to the design of Bentley, the text of the fourth century, which he supposed had been lost. For this purpose he laid aside all the later manuscripts, and confined himself to the few older ones. He also admitted the earliest Latin versions which existed before St. Jerome effected the Vulgate revision. And lastly, he employed the testimony of a few of the oldest Fathers.

Thus in the Gospels he had the guidance of the Alexandrian (A.), the Vatican (B.), the Parisian (C.), and four fragments,[1] besides an occasional use of the Cambridge manuscript (D):—the old Italian manuscript in Latin:—and the quotations of St. Irenæus, St. Cyprian, Origen, Lucifer, and Hilary. He made a clean sweep of all the rest,—a very satisfactory process as far as easiness of revision was concerned,—choosing a 'voluntary' and comfortable 'poverty' of materials, with a haughty disregard of the earnest labours of his predecessors.[2] Of his manuscripts, only one, the Vatican B, really conducted him into the fourth century, and of that he could then use only imperfect collations. The most important part of his work has been considered to be the toil which he expended upon the old Latin texts, and his vindication of their critical value, though that is not now held to be quite so high as his estimate would make it.

2. Lachmann was succeeded by Samuel Prideaux Tregelles, whose labours were much more prolific. Brought up

[1] P, Q, T, Z.
[2] Scrivener, "Plain Introduction," pp. 478, 9. Tregelles, "Printed Text," p. 104.

amongst the Society of Friends, he passed through the body of Plymouth Brethren into the position of a lay member of the Church of England.[1] The most important part of his work is to be found in his editions, and especially his collations of manuscripts. He edited two, the "Codex Zacynthius"(Ξ), belonging to the British and Foreign Bible Society, and the fragment O. He collated with great accuracy[2] eighteen Uncials, and thirteen Cursives. And he devoted much attention to Versions and Fathers, especially to Origen and Eusebius.[3]

He discussed Lachmann's method, in his "Account of the Printed Text of the New Testament," and accepted unreservedly the first principle. 'To Lachmann must be conceded this, that he led the way in casting aside the so-called Textus Receptus, and boldly placing the New Testament wholly and entirely on the basis of actual authority.'[4] With this utter disregard of the Received Text, Tregelles went on to the endorsement of the next principle, which was found in drawing a line of demarcation between the critical aids that are to be neglected as valueless, and those upon which dependence was to be placed. He divided manuscripts into three classes. The assent of those which were anterior to the seventh century was held by him to be essential for the settlement of any reading. The Cursives, dating since the tenth century, were erroneously regarded by him as in general opposed to the ancient copies. And the later Uncials, between the seventh and the eleventh centuries, appeared to him to be divided in their agreement between the modern and the ancient. So that the only trustworthy

---

[1] Scrivener, "Plain Introduction," p. 487.
[2] "Plain Introduction," p. 486.
[3] Ibid.   [4] "Printed Text," p. 99.

authorities were the oldest of these.[1] In a similar spirit, he attended to none but the earliest Versions, and to those sparingly, and cited no Fathers later than Eusebius in the earlier half of the fourth century. The reasons for this latter limit are : (1) because Eusebius 'is on the line of demarcation between the earlier text, and that which afterwards became widely diffused; and (2) because of the absolute necessity of confining such an examination between such limits as it might be practicable for one individual to reach in any moderate number of years.'[2] Tregelles died in 1875, before his Greek Testament was fully out.

3. But the most conspicuous figure in this school was Constantine Tischendorf, a man of the most remarkable energy and success, who in the services that he rendered in assembling materials for Textual Criticism, and in presenting them for employment to establish the genuineness of any reading, has out-topped even the most considerable figures in the long line of his predecessors. The eighth edition of his Greek Testament is an amazing monument of the incessant toil which occupied a life that ended on Dec. 7, 1874, shortly before the completion of his sixtieth year.

A record of his contributions to the critical aids to Textual Criticism has been given by Dr. Caspar Renè Gregory, who with some assistance from Professor Ezra Abbot, has written the first part of the "Prolegomena" to Tischendorf's Greek Testament. Tischendorf[3] discovered

---

[1] "Printed Text," p. 180. "Prolegomena to Greek New Testament," ix. He virtually rejected all Uncials later than the end of the sixth century, except L. X., Δ., Θ, and all Cursives whatever, except 1, 33, 69, *i.e.*, all that sided with the Textus Receptus.

[2] "Prolegomena," xviii. Horne and Tregelles "Introduction to the New Testament," p. 342. [3] P. 91.

fifteen Uncials, including the great Sinaitic manuscript (א), besides using for the first time twenty-three; he edited twenty-one, copied out four, and collated thirteen, not to reckon much labour spent upon more than thirty others, and toil of a smaller kind that is scarce recorded.

In the year 1844, whilst travelling under the patronage of Frederick Augustus King of Saxony, in quest of manuscripts, Tischendorf reached the Convent of St. Catherine, on Mount Sinai. Here observing some old-looking documents in a basketful of papers ready for lighting the stove, he picked them out, and discovered that they were forty-three vellum leaves of the Septuagint Version. He was allowed to take these: but in the desire of saving the other parts of the manuscript of which he heard, he explained their value to the monks, who being now enlightened would only allow him to copy one page, and refused to sell him the rest. On his return he published in 1846 what he had succeeded in getting, under the title of the "Codex Friderico-Augustanus," inscribed to his benefactor. In 1859, he was again in the East, being sent by Alexander II., Emperor of Russia, and was received at the convent as an emissary from the Great Protector of the Eastern Church. One night in a conversation with the steward, he was shewn a manuscript, 'written on loose leaves and wrapped in a red cloth,' and was allowed to examine it. He sat up all night with his treasure, for as he said, 'it seemed wicked to sleep.' He found a complete New Testament, a large portion of the Septuagint, the Epistle of St. Bárnabas, and a fragment of the Shepherd of Hermas. After this, he was allowed to copy the manuscript, and the Codex was in course of time presented to the Emperor, and is now at St. Petersburg.[1]

[1] "Christian Remembrancer," xlvi., p. 194. Scrivener's "Plain

Before the discovery of this important manuscript, Tischendorf had issued seven editions of his Greek Testament. In these, so far as the third, he had paid scarcely any attention to the Cursive manuscripts. After that edition, the course of his studies led him to introduce their record into his lists of authorities on passages. The consequence was that his seventh edition has been calculated to differ from the third in 1,296 instances, 'in no less than 595 of which (430 of the remainder being mere matters of spelling) he returned to the readings of the Received Text, which he had before deserted, but to which fresh materials and larger experience had brought him back.'[1] The eighth edition was constructed with the help of the newly discovered Sinaitic manuscript (א) and his attachment to the treasure that he had rescued proved too much for him. He altered his seventh edition in no less than 3,369 instances, generally in compliance with the Sinaitic copy, 'to the scandal,' as Dr. Scrivener justly remarks, 'of the science of Comparative Criticism, as well as to his own grave discredit for discernment and accuracy.'[2]

Much therefore as we may and must ever feel indebted to Tischendorf for the invaluable results of his labours, we cannot regard him as a man of sober and solid judgment. His zigzag course does not impress us with the soundness of any position upon which he found himself throughout it.

4. But the principles of this School of Textualists have reached their most complete exposition in the "Introduction to the Greek Testament," edited by Professors Westcott and Hort. This edition was founded upon labour in the case

Introduction, pp. 87, 88. Tischendorf, "Codex Sinaiticus, "Proleg.," p. xxii. Scrivener, "Codex Sinaiticus," vii—ix.

[1] Scrivener, "Plain Introduction," p. 529.   [2] Ibid.

of both those erudite men extending through nearly thirty years, including the period when as Revisers they were assisting in the Revision of the English Translation. Copies were however printed privately and placed in the hands of all the Revisers. It was not till the revision was out that they became public property. And shortly afterwards an elaborate and ingenious Introduction was published, from the hand, as is stated, of Dr. Hort.[1]

The object of the Introduction is evidently to reduce to a definite system the principles of Lachmann, and to advance grounds upon which the testimony of a few authorities standing by themselves may be accepted in preference to the verdict of the great majority of witnesses. Accordingly it is argued that a text which is found in the fourth century, although it was rejected and lay in all but oblivion throughout the succeeding ages,[2] is the genuine form and therefore must be followed. This doctrine leads to the exaltation of B and ℵ—but especially B[3]—into such an unique position, that after an examination of these principles and their application, an observer unacquainted with the history of manuscripts would imagine that these two very far surpassed all others both in antiquity and in an indisputable purity of expression. And indeed an attempt is made, based upon a large amount of speculation, but the very slenderest degree of evidence, to add a couple of centuries to their virtual age. But it must ever be remembered that A and C are nearly as ancient as B and ℵ. Indeed, one opinion makes

[1] P. 18. Yet it is true that, 'barely the smallest vestige of historical evidence has ever been alleged in support of the views of these accomplished editors.' Scrivener, "Plain Introduction," p. 531.

[2] Westcott and Hort, "Introduction," pp. 91, 92, 110, 142. Vol. i., pp. 547, 550.

[3] Westcott and Hort, "Introduction," pp. 171, 110.

A only about fifty years younger than B the eldest of the pair.¹ Besides which, according to dates now admitted, B and probably ℵ were produced under the dark gloom of Asian ascendency; A and C in the light of the most intellectual period of the early Church.

This deference to B, amounting almost to a superstitious adulation,² leads the two learned Professors to follow it whenever it is supported by only slight testimony from other quarters.³ Thus they adopt all the readings already enumerated in the Introduction to this little Treatise, and a vast number of others of the same kind.⁴

For example, they make St. Mark⁵ declare that the dancing-girl who demanded the head of John the Baptist was Herod Antipas' own daughter, and that her name was Herodias, in flat contradiction to the account in St. Matthew as edited by themselves, and at variance also with the history of the family, as given by Josephus.⁶ Again, the Lord is represented by them in St. Luke⁷ as preaching in the synagogues of Judea at the very time which He is said by St. Matthew and St. Mark to have spent in doing the same in the synagogues of Galilee, and when He ought to have been in the latter part of the Holy Land according to the context of the passage itself. Also in Acts x. 19, the Holy Spirit is described as telling St. Peter that two men were

---

¹ Cooke, "Revised Version," p. 185.
² Scrivener, "Plain Introduction," pp. 529, 530.
³ Westcott and Hort, "Introduction, 230-246.
⁴ Pp. 2, 3:—Occasionally, as in St. Luke xxii. 19, 20; xxiv. 3, 6, 9, 12, 36, 40, 52, even against the authority of B and ℵ.
⁵ St. Mark vi. 22. αὐτοῦ for αὐτῆς. The context in St. Mark is against this reading, which is besides ungrammatical.
⁶ St. Matt. xiv. 6. Josephus, "Antiq.," xviii., 5, §§. 1, 2, 4.
⁷ St. Luke iv. 44. Ἰουδαίας for Γαλιλαίας. St. Matt. iv. 23, St. Mark i. 39.

seeking Him, when the seventh verse had made it clear that there were three, viz., two of Cornelius' servants and a soldier who was his constant attendant.[1] And in Acts xii. 25, St. Paul and St. Barnabas are said to have returned from Jerusalem to Jerusalem, when they were really going back from Jerusalem to Antioch. Lastly,—not to make the specimen instances too numerous,—the Professors omit, and the Revisers too, 'the precious verse' (St. Matt. xvii. 21) 'which declares that this kind goeth not out but by prayer and fasting,' notwithstanding that only three manuscripts, B and ℵ and 33, testify by themselves for the omission against a very host of varied witnesses.[2]

This servile submission to B, in the face of copious testimony, may be also seen in their presentment of proper names. Such are Melitene for Melita, evidently a transcriptional blunder,[3] Nazara in two places only for Nazareth,[4] Beezebul for Beelzebul,[5] Joanes for Joannes,[6] the uncouth trunks Koum and Golgoth,[7] and—also a transcriptional mistake—the singular appellative Titius Justus.[8] They have also, with

---

[1] Also Acts xi. 11.

[2] Dean Burgon, "The Revision Revised," p. 91, 92, supplies these witnesses. Omission of verses is very common with these editors.

[3] ΜΕΛΙΤΗΗΝΗΣΟΣ. By eliding the article ἡ, and attaching the first syllable of νῆσος to Μελίτη. Acts xxviii. 1. See Burgon, "Revision Revised," p. 177. The letters in the oldest Uncial Manuscripts had no spaces between them.

[4] St. Matt. iv. 13: St. Luke iv. 16. They read elsewhere Ναζαρέθ and Ναζαρέτ.

[5] E.g. St. Matt. x. 25.

[6] Though only due to the scribe of B, i.e. also in the parts of ℵ written by that scribe. "Introduction," p. 159.

[7] St. Mark v. 41: St. Matt. xxvii. 33: St. Matt. xv. 22: St. John xix. 17.

[8] ΟΝΟΜΑΤΙΙΟΥΣΤΟΥ. Insert a second T between the last syl-

more reason and authority on their side, but with needless eccentricity, changed the order of Books, placing the Catholic Epistles before those of St. Paul.

To such results as these Professors Westcott and Hort have been guided in obedience to inexorable theory. Nevertheless, they have here and there sacrificed their consistency to some extent, as, for example, when they have shrunk from disfiguring St. Paul's exquisite description of Charity by the assertion that Charity 'seeketh not what is *not* her own,' and therefore that she adds to numerous sublime traits a freedom from gross violations of the eighth and tenth commandments. But this fitful courage does not keep them from admitting that such a bathos as this might possibly not have offended the inspired taste of St. Paul, inasmuch as they have placed in their margin this stupid blunder of the scribe of B.[1]

The Theory of the Cambridge Professors that leads to such results will be explained and sifted in the next chapter. But one feature in it must be noticed here. The authors adduce the slenderest support from actual evidence : ingenious as it is, their course of reasoning is ' entirely destitute of historical foundation.'[2] Dr. Hort gives no array of authorities in text or notes, and does not build up his theory upon acknowledged or produced facts.

The system thus unfolded has derived greater prominence from its having been mainly adopted by ' Two Members of the New Testament Company' in their defence of the

---

lable of ὀνόματι and the first two of 'Ιούστου, and Τιτίου is made immediately, and is due alone to B.

[1] οὐ ζητεῖ τὰ μὴ ἑαυτῆς after a faulty MS. used by Clement of Alexandria (252 Potter, 92 Migne), who, however (947 Potter, 345 Migne), gives the true words.

[2] Scrivener, "Plain Introduction," p. 537.

Revisers' Greek Text. No one can read their pamphlet,[1] or examine the readings admitted by a majority of the Revisers and defended by them, without seeing that, although their action is in some respects independent of Drs. Westcott and Hort, they generally uphold the principles advocated by those learned men. Indeed, alterations depending only upon B and ℵ, and sometimes upon B alone with some other support, are frequently preferred in the Revised Version before readings of the Textus Receptus, notwithstanding that the latter are so numerously and strongly attested, that on no other grounds except extreme deference to those Uncials could such a verdict be rejected.

The championship and support of men so learned and illustrious must carry great weight. And the question arises whether it be not so strong as to lead all who admire their great qualities to abide by their conclusions. Or is it possible, that as in the history of much human opinion, even they may have been induced to take a wrong turn in early days, and that they have been led into a valley attractive in itself but whence the best views have been excluded? Strange as such a conclusion might seem, the results of the present inquiry seem to point imperatively in no other direction. And such is the contention of men quite as eminent in this province as the upholders of the opinions just described.

IV. Signs of Coming Maturity.

Textual Criticism would not be governed by the principles that underlie all movements of human thought, if the strenuous pursuance of so limited a course as the one

---

[1] "The Revisers and The Greek Text of the New Testament," by Two Members of the New Testament Company, 1882.

recently followed did not provoke a departure in another direction. Accordingly strong opposition was made within the Revisers' Company by a stout minority headed by Dr. Scrivener the first textual critic of the day, and tacitly supported by Members of the Company who had ceased to act, as well as by other deep students of the subject, such as Dean Burgon and Canon Cook. And their advocacy has been developed into the teaching of a Rival and rising School, under which the basis is widened, and the building is being constructed out of all the materials within reach.

1. The labour spent by Dr. Scrivener upon Textual Criticism is well known from his admirable Introduction to the Science, a handbook [1] which leaves hardly anything, if anything, to be desired. Dr. Scrivener's candour, and patient and conscientious consideration of every point that presents itself, and of every opinion resting upon intelligence, are conspicuous in all that he has written upon this subject. And his accuracy, a matter of extreme importance in these matters, stands at the very top of editorial and collational work. 'Let the truth be told,' says the Dean of Chichester, 'C. F. Matthæi and he [*i.e.* Dr. Scrivener] are the only two scholars who have collated any considerable number of sacred codices with the needful amount of accuracy.' [2]

In 1853, Dr. Scrivener published 'A full and exact Collation of about twenty Greek manuscripts of the Holy Gospels.' In his Introduction he said : 'The following pages comprise a humble yet earnest attempt to revive among the countrymen of Bentley and Mill some interest in a branch of

---

[1] "A Plain Introduction to the Criticism of the New Testament for the use of Biblical Students," by F. H. A. Scrivener, M.A., D.C.L., LL.D., &c., 3rd edition, 1883.

[2] "The Revision Revised," p. 246.

Biblical learning which, for upwards of a century, we have tacitly abandoned to continental scholars.' The success of this attempt, if limited in these earlier days of Dr. Scrivener's influence to comparatively a small band of scholars, nevertheless has been conspicuous. This work was followed in 1859 by 'An exact Transcript of the Codex Augiensis . . . to which is added a Full Collection of Fifty Manuscripts.' To both of these works valuable Introductions are prefixed, explanatory of the principles of the Science, and containing discussions upon controverted questions, such as whether there are families of Manuscripts, and against the partial use of only a few authorities, as advocated by Lachmann and Tregelles. In 1864, he published 'A Full Collation of the Codex Sinaiticus' (א), with corrections of errata in Tischendorf's editions of the same manuscript. And in the same year he edited for the University of Cambridge a handsome volume containing the great Cambridge manuscript (D). Such, with his 'Plain Introduction' already noticed, have been his chief, but by no means his only works.

The line taken by Dr. Scrivener has uniformly been that all evidence must be employed in comparative or Textual Criticism. Yet not all indiscriminately; but each being assigned its proper value. Thus he by no means accedes to the proposal of neglecting the Received Text. But, on the other hand, he has ever admitted that revision is required, and has been ready to submit to the clear verdict of evidence. He would proceed with far-sighted and wide-viewed caution; and would urge that everything possible should be done to make all documents of whatever sort ready to minister in their several places to well-pondered conclusions.

2. Of about the same age as Dr. Scrivener, but in the enjoyment of better health, the Dean of Chichester is a re-

doubtable champion upon the same side. His first Book in this department was a vindication of "The Last Twelve Verses of St. Mark's Gospel," published in 1871, in which according to the award of the first living judge, he 'has thrown a stream of light upon the controversy, nor does the joyous tone of his book misbecome one who is conscious of having triumphantly maintained a cause which is very precious to him.' Even so unfavourable a judge as Mr. Hammond admits the cogency and success of his arguments.[1] Another, marked with the natural impetuosity of Dean Burgon's controversial style, but bristling with learning, and built upon remarkably strong and detailed foundations, which, as it appears, many of his opponents have not the patience to examine accurately, is "The Revision Revised," a republication of Articles in the "Quarterly Review," with additions, chiefly upon the disputed text in the First Epistle to St. Timothy.[2] Besides these books the Dean is constantly at work, and is believed to have copious materials for future publication. And his "Letters from Rome" (1862), and sundry letters from time to time in the "Guardian" newspaper, as well as contributions to editions of Dr. Scrivener's "Plain Introduction," to the last of which he has added particulars of three hundred and seventy-four manuscripts previously unknown to the world of letters, are results of toil which has been continued for many years.

Dean Burgon has incurred much misrepresentation. He does not maintain the faultlessness of the Received Text; he is not a devoted adherent of the Alexandrian Codex (A);

---

[1] "Outlines of Textual Criticism," &c., by C. E. Hammond, M.A., 3rd ed., pp. 116-23.

[2] 1 Timothy iii. 16. Θεός instead of the advocated ὅς or ὅ. See below, "Appendix," vii.

he does not simply count his authorities, or follow the largest number, irrespectively of their weight and value. But he urges that all should be taken into account; 'that the Truth of the Text of Scripture is to be elicited exclusively from the consentient testimony of the largest number of the best Copies, Fathers, Versions;'[1] that that is the Truth which 'enjoys the earliest, the fullest, the widest, the most respectable, and—above all things—the most varied attestation;'[2] that all the existing Copies must be assembled and accurately collated, the Versions edited, and the Fathers indexed before a revision of the Greek Text can be successfully accomplished;[3] that evidence and examination prove convincingly that the Vatican (B) and the Sinaitic (ℵ) manuscripts exhibit really bad, instead of good, texts;[4] and that all must be rested upon definite external attestation, not upon the shifting sands of conjecture, opinion, taste, and other internal sources of inference.[5] It should be added, that Dean Burgon surpasses everyone in acquaintance with Patristic evidence of readings.

3. Another learned maintainer of this view of the controversy is Canon Cook, the editor in chief of the "Speaker's Commentary." His controversy with the Bishop of Durham upon the rendering of the last petition in the Lord's Prayer, on which his last and longest letter has remained as yet unanswered, and his treatise upon the "Revised Version of the First Three Gospels," have been important contributions to the literature of this subject. Calm, moderate, weighty in argument, learned, persuasive, he has controverted the main positions of the opposed School in the latter of these two

---

[1] "The Revision Revised," p. 518.
[2] Ibid., p. 339.
[3] Ibid., pp. 125, 247, note.
[4] Ibid., pp. 11-17, 249, 262-265.
[5] Ibid., pp. 19-20, 253.

works with great cogency. He maintains that the Vatican (B) and Sinaitic (א) Codices have been unduly exalted; that the Alexandrian (A), which in the Gospels fairly represents the text used by St. Chrysostom and his great contemporaries, is superior to them; that the former two were probably written under the direction of Eusebius; and that the theories and arguments of Drs. Westcott and Hort are destitute of solid foundation.

Also those eminent Scholars, Bishops Christopher and Charles Wordsworth—' Par nobile Fratrum '—the loss of the first of whom we are now deploring,[1] have spoken upon the same side in Charges delivered to the Clergy of their Dioceses, deprecating amongst other things ' too much confidence in certain favourite manuscripts.'[2]

Nor is this contention without contemporary support upon the Continent. In 1862, Dr. J. G. Reiche warned scholars against the dangerous principles introduced by Lachmann, and the almost superstitious veneration that was then paid to Lachmann's text. And especially he spoke against the practice introduced by that learned scholar of consulting only a few witnesses, observing especially that several of the Versions are older than any manuscripts.[3] In 1860, writing from Leyden, A. Kuenen and C. G. Cobet, in the Preface to an

[1] Bp. Chr. Wordsworth, Charge, Nov. 1881.
[2] I cannot pass on without a tribute to the fearless faithfulness, the vast mass of learning ever at hand, the open munificence, and the administrative capacity of that great man.

' Cui Pudor, et Justitiæ soror,
Incorrupta Fides, nudaque Veritas,
Quando ullum invenient parem ? '

[3] " Commentarius Criticus," Tomus iii. Ep. ad Heb. et Ep. Cath. continens. Observatio prævia. Cook, " Revised Version," pp. 4-7. Burgon, " The Revision Revised," pp. 380-81.

edition of the Vatican Codex, protested against the notion that because that was the oldest manuscript it therefore possessed an authority paramount to that of all others. On the contrary, they asserted, proving the assertion with a copious array of evidence, that 'there is no kind of error that is not frequently found in that manuscript as in all the rest.'[1] Also at the beginning of 1884, Dr. J. H. A. Michelsen, in the "Theologisch Tijdschrift," a monthly magazine published at Leyden, submitted the text of B and א to a vigorous examination. From internal proofs, such as glosses introduced from other passages, readings plainly bad where better exist, and omissions of verses and paragraphs, all copiously illustrated, he drew the conclusion that the so-called Neutral Text is not so good as the advocates of it claim, and directed attention to the dangerous traversing of the principle, 'Quod semper, quod ubique, quod ab omnibus,' which is involved in the acceptance of that form of Text.

Besides these, we may reckon the strong sentiment prevailing in the Roman Branch of the Church. Vercellone, the editor of B, now no more, held no such opinions as those of Extreme Textualism. Ceriani, of Milan, and a learned writer in the "Dublin Review,"[2] seem to represent what is held in those quarters. And the Abbè Martin, of Paris, in his elaborate "Fascicules" maintains the same side of the controversy.

It will be seen from this sketch, that so far from questions being already settled amongst the learned and ripe for a general decision which would enjoy universal assent, two Rival Schools are now contending for the ascendency.

---

[1] "Novum Testamentum, ad fid. Cod. Vat., ed. A. Kuenen et C. G. Cobet," Præfatio, p. xiii. &c.

[2] Jan. 1884. On "New Testament Vaticanism."

THE TWO RIVAL SCHOOLS. 37

The one, of German origin, is strongly and ably maintained in England, and reckons large support amongst Biblical Scholars. The other, headed by the first Textual Critic of the day, and earnestly advocated by accomplished Theologians, counts also among its adherents Roman Catholics in England and on the Continent, including experts in Italy and elsewhere. Therefore careful and respectful consideration is further necessary, in order that after contrasting and weighing the several characteristics of both Schools, we may know from solid considerations which of the two to follow.

CHAPTER IV.

THE SCHOOL OF EXTREME TEXTUALISM.

THEORY OF WESTCOTT AND HORT EXPLAINED AND REFUTED.

A NEW period began in 1831, when for the first time a text was constructed directly from the ancient documents without the intervention of any printed edition, and when the first systematic attempt was made to substitute scientific method for arbitrary choice in the discrimination of various readings.' So the leading masters in the First of the Rival Schools attribute its foundation to Lachmann.[1] Drs. Westcott and Hort began with Lachmann's principles,[2] and after many years have brought them to their natural and extreme development in the elaborate system which they have constructed, and which is in the main accepted and upheld by other adherents of this School.[3]

Therefore the chief characteristics of the teaching of this School, so far as they have been hitherto unfolded in public, may be derived from Dr. Hort's elaborate Introduction.

So far as they are peculiar to the School, they are susceptible of classification under the following heads :—Internal

---

[1] Westcott and Hort, "Introduction," p. 13.

[2] Ibid., p. 16.

[3] So the two members of the Revisers' Company ; Professor Sanday in the "Contemporary Review," Dec. 1881 ; Archdeacon Farrar, "Expositor," 1882 ; and a writer in the "Church Quarterly," Jan. 1882.

Evidence, Genealogy, Families or Groups, the worthlessness of the Syrian Text (so-called), and the super-eminent excellence of B and the other representatives of the (so-termed) Neutral Text.[1]

1. In dealing with the divergent evidence which is constantly presented in different passages, two main considerations, so Dr. Hort tells us, offer themselves, viz., Which is in itself the most probable reading? and, What is the character of the documents by which it is supported? Now a reading may in the first place be recommended by its own likelihood. It may make better sense than the rival word, or phrase, or clause, or sentence. It may be more in keeping with the author's style of writing, or his matter of composition, as gathered from other passages. But Dr. Hort lays no stress on all this, and urges that the most important part of what is called Internal Evidence consists in acquaintance with the character of the Documents themselves in which the readings are found. Hence his first principle:—
'Knowledge of Documents should precede Final Judgments upon Readings.'

Now the character of a Document, he says, depends, (*a*) chiefly upon its date, (*b*) next upon the purity or corruption of its text. The character of the text may be discovered by a large comparison of its readings with other ascertained readings, according to careful methods.[2] Judged in this manner, the Vatican MS. especially, and the Sinaitic also, are predominant, not only by reason of their un-

---

[1] These terms, Syrian, Alexandrian, Neutral, as used by the two Professors, can only be employed under protest, till they can be proved to have anything but an imaginary existence.

[2] Westcott and Hort, "Introduction," pp. 30-39. The entire account is too involved to give here.

rivalled antiquity, but also because of the excellence of their text.

2. But now, as Dr. Hort argues, another important factor comes into sight. Scribes transcribed from documents, and thus one document became the parent of the next. So we are introduced to the use of arguments derived from Genealogy. 'All trustworthy restoration of corrupted texts is founded upon the study of their history, that is of the relations of descent or affinity which connect the several documents.'[1] In this way, one manuscript may be found, as Dr. Hort thinks, to have proceeded from another, and the weight of authority from both becomes only the weight of authority possessed by the earlier of the two. Again, two or more documents are observed to be so similar to one another that they must have been transcribed either directly, or through one or more intervening ancestors, from a common original. Accordingly, their united authority, how many soever they are, does not exceed the authority of their single original. But 'identity of reading implies identity of origin;' and the outlines of such a common original may be deciphered in the resemblances of manuscripts, and the purity of a text inferred in discarding individual traces of corruption. Thus Dr. Hort concludes, upon close examination, that B and ℵ were derived from a common original much older than themselves, 'the date of which cannot be later than the early part of the second century, and may well be yet earlier.' This would bring our chief documentary authority nearly back to the Apostolic autographs, and would invest it with paramount importance.

3. The same conclusion is reached by Dr. Hort from a consideration of the families or groups into which docu-

---

[1] Westcott and Hort, "Introduction," p. 40.

ments are divided by him. History shews that one mainly uniform text has prevailed from the present time as far back as the second half of the fourth century. This he denominates the 'Syrian' text (i.), which he declares to have derived its origin from a recension made at Antioch, and to have come thence to Constantinople, since Antioch was the 'true ecclesiastical parent of Constantinople.'[1] Enthroned thus in the Eastern capital, it became dominant in the Christian world. But there are said by him to have been three other texts 'which can be identified through numerous readings distinctively attested by characteristic groups of extant documents.' These are called by Dr. Hort (ii.) the Western, which was found in Italy, Africa, and other parts of the West, as well as originally in Syria, and dealt largely in paraphrase and interpolation, as may be seen in the Cambridge Codex Bezæ (D), its chief existing representative; (iii.) the Alexandrian, of which but little evidence remains; and (iv.) the Neutral, which is free from the peculiarities of either, and of which there are traces, 'indubitable and significant,' 'in the remains of Clement and Origen, together with the fragment of Dionysius and Peter of Alexandria,' and 'in a certain measure in the works of Eusebius of Cæsarea, who was deeply versed in the theological literature of Alexandria.'[2]

4. It appears, therefore, Dr. Hort continues, that of these four types of text, two are affected with peculiar traces of corruption, viz., the Western which degenerated into paraphrase, and 'incorporation of extraneous matter,' and the Alexandrian, which is oppressed with minor faults, such as 'incipient paraphrase and skilful assimilation.' The Neutral alone of the remaining two reached back to earliest times.

---

[1] Westcott and Hort, "Introduction," p. 143.   [2] Ibid., p. 127.

The Syrian is represented as worthless, because it was made up in the fourth century, as is attempted to be proved in the following manner:—

(1.) The analysis of certain passages, of which eight are given, is declared by Dr. Hort to prove that the 'Syrian' Text was made up by an eclectic combination of the readings of other texts into one 'conflate' reading. For instance, in St. Mark vi. 33, at the end of the verse, the 'Neutral' reading is said to be καὶ προῆλθον αὐτούς, the 'Western' συνῆλθον αὐτοῦ, both of which are supposed to be combined in the 'Syriac' into καὶ προῆλθον αὐτούς, καὶ συνῆλθον πρὸς αὐτόν. Dr. Hort argues at some length that the last phrase spoils St. Mark's diction. And from this and similar instances he draws the conclusion that at some authoritative revision the other texts were blended into a 'form lucid and complete, smooth and attractive, but appreciably impoverished in sense and force, more fitted for cursory perusal or recitation than for repeated and diligent study.'

(2.) The same conclusion is supposed to be reached by the evidence of the Ante-Nicene Fathers, none of whom—it is contended—exhibit a 'Syrian' Text. The Latin Fathers, of course, quote the Western; and they are said to be followed by Justin Martyr, Irenæus, Hippolytus, Methodius, and Eusebius.[1] In the works of Clement of Alexandria, it is maintained that non-Western as well as Western quotations are discoverable, but no 'Syrian;' and in those of Origen all the other kinds of texts can be found, but none, Dr. Hort thinks, of a distinctively 'Syrian' character.

(3.) This position, as Dr. Hort argues, is confirmed by

---

[1] Westcott and Hort, "Introduction," p. 113.

the internal evidence of various passages, though it is admitted that the authors of the 'Syrian' Text 'may have copied from some other equally ancient and perhaps purer text now otherwise lost.'[1] But Dr. Hort says that examination shews that this text was made up by revisers from the rest, sometimes by following one or other, sometimes by modification, or by combination, or pruning, or by introducing changes of their own when they had none to follow.[2]

Hence, Dr. Hort concludes that 'all distinctively Syrian readings may be set aside at once as certainly originating after the middle of the third century, and therefore, as far as transmission is concerned, corruptions of the apostolic text.' He even asserts that they can attest nothing by themselves, and do not always add strength to attestations of the other texts, because they may themselves be only derived from the original autographs through those very texts.

5. It follows, he thinks, that the Neutral, where it can be verified, remains as alone the pure representative of the unalloyed Scriptures of the New Testament. It has been already declared that, in his opinion, B and ℵ, the leading MSS. which set forth this text, enjoy a special pre-eminence, because of their superior antiquity, and by reason of their purity of text.

Accordingly, with slight exception, 'readings of ℵ B should be accepted as the true readings until strong internal evidence is found to the contrary, and no readings of ℵ B can safely be rejected absolutely, though it is sometimes right to place them only on an alternative footing, especially where they receive no support from Versions or Fathers.' Of the two, B is the purer, which 'must be regarded as having preserved

---

[1] Westcott and Hort, "Introduction," p. 115.   [2] Ibid., p. 118.

not only a very ancient text, but a very pure line of very ancient text,'[1] א having on its way fallen upon 'at least two early aberrant texts.'[2] When therefore B stands with any other leading manuscript alone without א, its readings nearly always 'have the ring of genuineness.'[3] And 'even when B stands quite alone, its readings must never be lightly rejected.'[4]

Such, so far as the present limits will admit, are the leading points in the Theory of Drs. Westcott and Hort. If it has been improperly portrayed, this is not due to any want of desire to do justice to it.

And indeed even what has been here said, and still more the elaborate treatises in the Introduction and at the end of the text of the Greek Testament, must impress all persons deeply with the patient ingenuity, the critical acumen, and the mastery of the subject evinced by those distinguished scholars.

But whether this Theory has a strong and solid foundation, and will endure the shock of the long examination and vigorous analysis that it is sure to encounter, or indeed whether it has any foundation at all, is quite another matter. The solution which it offers in all difficulties is too suspiciously easy. It almost amounts to this:—'Do not trouble yourself about other authorities, but attend to B and א, which will supply all you want.' How can it be right to cast to the winds at least four-fifths of the evidence—if it be not vastly more—and to draw the inferences solely from the remainder? Such a course cannot but carry with it its own condemnation. And on studying and testing the Theory, the first thing that strikes a man of logical mind is, that he sees an

---

[1] Westcott and Hort, "Introduction," p. 251. [2] Ibid., p. 249.
[3] Ibid., p. 227. [4] Ibid., Preface, p. 557.

ambitious and lofty outline, which upon closer examination turns out to be merely cloud reared upon cloud. There is no firm footing for the feet of an inquirer. The impalpable and shadowy nature of the investigation contrasts strangely with the gravity and earnestness of the writer. There is abundance of considerations, surmises, probabilities, generalizations, made both from known particulars of history and from details lying in the memories or in the private note-books of the authors; but an array of facts strong enough to establish satisfactorily each stage in advance is wholly wanting, whilst the leaps made in ardent speculation here and there over wide chasms reveal the insecurity of the country traversed. Proofs are required : and no real proofs are offered. Seldom indeed has a theory been advanced with so few facts for its basis.

Passing now to the examination of the general considerations that are presented, we find too little stress laid upon such Internal Evidence as is grounded upon clear facts or sound sense, and too much upon a classification of documents which rests exclusively upon individual opinion. The real judge of Internal Evidence is the sanctified intellect, applying the conclusions, not of separate minds of a peculiar cast; not of single schools of opinion neutralized by other schools, but of the corporate thought of the Church, resting upon a clear foundation of sense or fact, ascertained in a vigorous exercise of mental power. And the illumination of the sanctified intellect proceeds from the Great Inspirer of the Holy Scriptures themselves, the true Interpreter of their form and meaning, the Source of all the mental strength in the world, the Holy Spirit of the Eternal God. But we do not hear from the Extreme Textualist School of any such judgment, and so they leave their common sense behind them, and we are told that the Lord's side was pierced before death, that the sun was eclipsed when the moon was full, and that it is possible that St. Paul may have added to the high traits of Charity that she actually refrains from seeking what is not her own. On the other hand, such inferences as are drawn from the natural or known proclivities of copyists must be employed sparingly, and cannot support much weight in the face of positive attestation. And judgments upon the Internal character of documents, unless generally accepted within the boundaries of the Science, or supported by definite, produced, clear reasons, cannot be accepted as foundations to build upon. Even pure antiquity, when evidence is scanty, is too rude an instrument of relative decision. The comparative assessment of the value of ancient origin is not of necessity measured by centuries or decades, because some of the associations of the earliest ages were far from good, and any document may reflect them, whilst another of later date may be more free from such disturbing influences. We do not go back merely to Ante-Nicene times for the Canon of Scripture, or we might find cause to include the Epistle of St. Barnabas in the list of books. At the same time, if we light upon a pure strain of the best antiquity, we cannot fail to be on the right track. Again, there may be a great variety of opinions upon the purity of any text. Drs. Westcott and Hort, and others, rate B and ℵ very high. It may perhaps be more than doubted whether such would be the verdict of critics, if they approached them without knowing what they were. Dr. Scrivener, in his calm and dispassionate manner, places the estimate some way down. Dean Burgon, upon plain and definite grounds, rates them very low. Kuenen and Cobet say that B is full of errors. Till agreement is reached, it is evident that reasons so shifting and unstable can constitute no real pillar of support for any superstructure.[1]

Next of Genealogy. Here evidently lurk the pitfalls which are involved in an analogy made the groundwork of an argument. The reasoning is correct, so far as it is impossible for a good copy to be made from a bad exemplar, though to a slight extent external influence, such as the recollection in the copyist of a better guide, may somewhat improve the offspring, like good companionship or the effects of study; or secondly, as to the probability that better as well as worse features will be reproduced in the copies made from it. Again, we are told that, 'so far as genealogical relations are discovered with perfect certainty,' 'being directly involved in historical facts,' 'their immediate basis is historical, not speculative.'[2] But indeed inasmuch as 'no single step in the descent can be produced, in other words, no genealogical evidence exists,'[3] all is precarious instead of

---

[1] Dr. Hort goes so far as to admit the use of conjectural emendation. ("Introd.," p. 7.) Well may Dean Burgon say, 'Conjectural Emendation can be allowed no place whatever in the Textual Criticism of the New Testament.' This is an established principle (Scrivener, "Plain Introduction," p. 490-1.) It is too dangerous an instrument in the hand of any man, and wholly devoid of authority, which is of the essence of Holy Writ. Besides, the wealth of illustration makes it scarce anywhere needed. "When . . . it was clear that the channels of transmission was sufficient to supply evidence on the text, there was no one thing as to which critical editors were more unanimous than in the rejection of all conjecture in the formation of a text."—Tregelles, "Introduction to the Critical Study," &c., pp. 149, 150.

[2] Westcott and Hort, "Introduction," p. 63.

[3] Dean Burgon, "The Revision Revised," p. 256. The Dean further shows (p. 257) that close relationship is known only in three instances, (1) F. and G. ; (2) 13, 69, 124, and 346 ; and (3) B and ℵ ; and that these are related as brothers (or sisters) or cousins, not in

being historical, and there are no premisses and therefore no inference. Between the actual facts and the supposed conclusion often lies a long space into which speculation is but too apt to enter.

For instance, when Dr. Hort argues that the similarity to one another of those numerous Uncials in what he terms the Syrian class shows that they came from one ancestor, and that although they largely outnumber ℵ and B, they can therefore have at the best only the authority of one ancestor set against another ancestor, he entirely disregards the presumption that a larger number of descendants came from a larger number of ancestors, and that the majority may be only thrust back from one generation to a previous one. In truth, the argument from genealogy—such as it is—conducts the unprejudiced inquirer to results the very opposite to those of Dr. Hort.

Again, when it is assumed that the common ancestor of ℵ and B came into existence in the early part of the second century, there is, so far as genealogy is concerned, a lofty disregard of the obvious truth that generations might be propagated as fast as the pens of scribes would admit; and that after the wholesale destruction of copies in the persecution of Diocletian and Galerius, it is almost certain that transcription must have proceeded at a rapid rate. Genealogy therefore is misleading, for it supplies no warrant for any conclusion as to time, and in fact suggests an untrue analogy. If on other grounds this is a speculative inference, the instinct of such experienced scholars as Drs. Westcott and Hort is entitled to respectful consideration. But it

---

any direct line of genealogy. To these three instances must now be added, since the discovery of Σ, the affinity between Σ and N. Scrivener, "Plain Introduction," p. 159.

cannot be endorsed by other students than themselves, until it is proved to have foundation in well-authenticated facts duly represented.

But the principle of Genealogy must be regarded on the side of descendants as well as of ancestors. Manuscripts in high repute ought to have been largely copied. Was the great era of Chrysostom, of Basil, of the Gregories, when the Canon of Scripture was settled, and the Faith of Christendom fixed, so innocent of the value of pure Texts, that the learned let the true type preserved in at least two preeminently good ones languish in obscurity and disuse? Yet whilst the other form of Text numbers its many hundreds, Dr. Hort reckons only twelve Neutral MSS. in all of the Gospels.[1] Can this fact be accounted anything else than a deliberate and unremitting condemnation of the two documents under investigation? Incidental proofs are not wanting that the character of disputed passages and of manuscripts came under careful discussion during this and the succeeding ages.[2] It is inconceivable that, amidst the wealth of dissident documents, and at a time when the literary intellect of the world was occupied with ecclesiastical questions, and the monuments of past authorship were being stored, there could have existed such neglect of the purity of the sacred writings of the Church as is taken for granted by Dr. Hort. The abundance of contemporary commentaries forbids such a supposition. Therefore the Vatican and Sinaitic manuscripts cannot but receive very serious discredit from their want of following.

[1] Westcott and Hort, "Introduction," p. 171. These are B, ℵ, 'T of St. Luke and St. John, Ξ of St. Luke, L., 33, Δ (in St. Mark), C, Z of St. Matthew, R of St. Luke, Q, and·P.'

[2] See below, Chapter VII.

Again, the theory of Families, or groups, of manuscripts cannot stand in any definite or clearly cut shape. Since it was first proposed by Bentley, it has passed through constant modifications. The foundations laid by one master have been disturbed by his successor, whose own excavations and masses of cement have been re-made by the next. The difficulties to which the constructors of an inexorable theory have been driven are shown by the severing of one manuscript, after the example of Solomon's award, into portions supposed to belong to three Families. Dr. Scrivener is surely right in describing this process as 'that violent and most unlikely hypothesis, that Cod. A follows the Byzantine class of authorities in the Gospels, the Western in the Acts and Catholic Epistles, and the Alexandrian in St. Paul.'[1]

But it may be asked, is there then no truth at all in the assignment of characters to manuscripts, or in any sort of grouping? And the answer of a candid inquirer must be that there may perhaps be an amount of justice in the connotation of characteristic features, but that great care must be taken not to lay too much stress upon it, and certainly not to draw a few broad and dark lines separating one province from another. And especially, generalizations constructed upon such induction as the case admits, must be employed most sparingly in deductive arguments, or logic will stand aghast.

And as to the Families, òr groups, suggested by Dr. Westcott and Hort, there are no doubt a number of documents

---

[1] "Plain Introduction," p. 472. 'Quæ cum ita sint, sequitur exercentibus rem criticam summa opus esse cautione in adhibenda classium sive recensionum distinctione : quam ut summam normam aut fundamentum ponere et temerarium et frustra est.'—Tischendorf, quoted by Dr. Caspar Renè Gregory, Prolegomena, 1884, p. 196.

which ordinarily support the Traditional Text, there are also others which make for what they call the Neutral Text, and others which support Western readings. And there are many that take different sides : and most of those which are generally found on one, occasionally appear on the other. There are also Western readings and Alexandrian readings. But the existence of an 'Alexandrian' text, as distinct from their 'Neutral' text, is more than doubtful. Dr. Hort's description of it is of the vaguest, and the materials of proof, which are all that he can point to, are of the scantiest.

We now come to the position resting upon the supposed posteriority of the so-called Syrian Text. Here again we are in the region of pure speculation unsustained by historical facts. Dr. Hort imagines first that there was a recension of the early Syrian Version, which this School maintains was represented by the Curetonian Version, somewhere between 250, A.D., and 350, at Edessa, or Nisibis, or Antioch.[1] The result of this recension is said to have been the Peshito Version, which has hitherto been referred to the second century. We may remark, by the way, that the Peshito must be got rid of by Extreme Textualists, or it would witness inconveniently before the Fourth century to the 'Syrian' Text. Well indeed may Dr. Hort add 'even for conjecture the materials are scanty.' It would have been truer to the facts to have said, 'for such a conjecture there are no materials at all, and therefore it must be abandoned.'[2]

But Drs. Westcott and Hort also maintain that an authoritative recension of a much larger character was made after

---
[1] Westcott and Hort, "Introduction," pp. 136, 137.
[2] See Dr. Scrivener, "Plain Introduction," pp. 233-4, and Dean Burgon's elaborate proof of the groundlessness of the supposition of any authoritative recension at all, in "The Revision Revised," pp. 272-281.

this at Antioch, and resulted in the formation of the 'Syrian' Text of the Gospels in Greek, which was formed upon the Vulgate, or common Syriac Version. What proof exists anywhere of such an important proceeding? A recension, be it observed, so thorough and so sweeping in its effects, that, according to the theory under consideration, it must have placed the text it produced in such a commanding situation that it has reigned for fifteen centuries without a rival. How could this have occurred without an achievement so great and famous that the report of it must have gone abroad? Surely this must have been another Council of Nicæa, or at least a Council of Ariminum. Such results could not have issued from a mystery like that of the viewless wind. Yet there is positively no record in the history—not to speak of a Council of the Church—but of any single incident justifying the assumption that such an authoritative revision ever took place.[1] Never surely was there such an attempt before made to foist such pure fiction into history. But besides that, the arguments for the formation of a new text in the Fourth century thoroughly break down.

(1.) The evidence in only the eight[2] instances given is certainly not enough to establish the existence of such a 'conflation,' or a combination of supposed other texts into one eclectic reading throughout the New Testament. But supposing for a moment that these eight were specimens of what constantly occurs, who, from internal evidence alone, can say dogmatically which is posterior—the entire text, or the respective portions of it? Surely the integral whole,

---

[1] See Burgon's, "The Revision Revised," pp. 272-88; and Cook's "Revised Version," pp. 195-204. Dr. Scrivener calls the two supposed recensions 'phantom revisions.' "Plain Introduction," p. 534.

[2] Westcott and Hort, Introduction.

which Dr. Hort (p. 134) admits to possess 'lucidity and completeness,' and to be 'entirely blameless on either literary or religious grounds as regards vulgarized or unworthy diction,' has the better title to be held to have been the original form than any of the separate portions. Omission must be a possible fault with all copyists;[1] and indubitable instances show that the scribes of ℵ and B were habitual offenders in this respect. With reference to the character of the texts, many scholars would not agree with Drs. Westcott and Hort in the value which they set upon a Thucydidean ruggedness.[1]

(2.) As to the alleged absence of readings of the Traditional Text from the writings of the Ante-Nicene Fathers, Dr. Hort draws largely upon his imagination and his wishes. The persecution of Diocletian is here also the parent of much want of information. But is there really such a dearth of these readings in the works of the Early Fathers as is supposed? Dr. Scrivener[3] maintains that Dr. Hort speaks much too sweepingly. Besides this, Dean Burgon has cited against the readings advocated by the New School more than fifty authorities from Ante-Nicene writings upon five passages.[4] Are these ten testimonies on an average to each

---

[1] St. Jerome traces transcriptional error to three sources:—
    (1) Vel a vitiosis interpretibus male edita,
    (2) Vel a presumptoribus imperitis emendata perversius,
    (3) Vel a librariis dormitantibus addita sunt.'
    Præfatio ad Damasum.

[2] See note at the end of the chapter.

[3] "Plain Introduction," pp. 533-540.

[4] Last twelve verses of St. Mark; 1 Tim. iii. 16; St. Luke xxii. 43, 44; xxiii. 34; ii. 14. 'The number of Early Fathers,' ending always with Eusebius, is about 100. Burgon, "Last Twelve Verses," p. 21; "The Revision Revised," p. 290. See below, Chapter VI., end. Dean Burgon's command of Patristic evidence is simply mar-

passage to be reckoned as alien to the Traditional Text, or not rather as evident indications of an earlier origin reaching back to the Apostolic age? Besides the Fathers, some of the Versions—notably the Peshito, which is referred by the best critics to the second century [1]—that are older than any MSS., give frequent support to the readings of the Traditional Text.

(3.) What is said about Internal Evidence is much too vague and misty to sustain so strong a conclusion. And it is balanced with the candid admission, that after all the peculiar readings of the Received Text may perhaps be derived from 'some equally ancient and perhaps purer text now otherwise lost.'[2] What seems to Dr. Westcott and Dr. Hort to constitute internal evidence in each instance does not seem so to others. Where is the rock amidst this perilous sand-drift?

We are driven therefore to the characters of ℵ and B as the last refuge of the Theory under examination.

And we cannot but be struck with the great argument in their favour. They are the oldest MSS. in existence. They are extremely handsome, and in some respects are complete.[3] Their verdict in the opinion of nearly all judges is entitled to respectful attention.

But besides that they are not much older than A and C, how can Drs. Westcott and Hort get over the central fact that these MSS. have hardly any following in the ages after

---

vellous. It is to be hoped that he will communicate to the Church the treasures that he must have been long amassing.

[1] See below, Chapter VI.
[2] Westcott and Hort, "Introduction," p. 115.
[3] ℵ is the only complete Uncial copy of the New Testament. B ends at Heb. ii. 14, but is complete so far, except in its numerous omissions.

them, and so have been condemned by Catholic antiquity? They were probably produced about A.D. 330-340,[1] a short time before the Canon of Holy Scripture was settled, when the general subject of the Holy Scriptures must have come under discussion. They just antedated the most intelligent period of the early Church, when the finest intellects in the world were engaged in ascertaining the exact lineaments of 'The Faith once delivered to the saints.' How could these men have escaped from spending particular care upon the Sacred Text? We learn that St. Jerome did so upon the Latin Versions. And the fact, acknowledged over and over again by Dr. Hort, that one uniform text has prevailed from that period till now, surely alone constitutes a decisive condemnation of this so-called 'Neutral Text.'

The period too of the production of these two MSS. is instructive. It was when the Church was all but Semiarian: of this there is no doubt. But it appears also extremely probable that they were made under the direction of Eusebius of Cæsarea, a leader of the Semiarian party. The scribe of the Vatican B is supposed by Tischendorf, with the agreement of Dr. Scrivener and by the admission of Dr. Hort, to have written part of the Sinaitic ℵ.[2] The date of the execution, as fixed upon other grounds, was about the time when Eusebius was commissioned by Constantine to prepare fifty manuscripts of the Holy Scriptures, and send them to Constantinople. These two MSS. stand unrivalled for the beauty of their caligraphy, and of the vellum on which they are written, and in all respects are just what we should expect

---

[1] See Cook, "Revised Version," p. 160.

[2] *I.e.*, 'six conjugate leaves of Cod. ℵ, being three pairs in three distant quires, one of them containing the conclusion of St. Mark's Gospel.' "Plain Introduction," p. 92, note 1.

to have been produced in obedience to an imperial mandate.[1]

And, as has been already stated, the text of these two manuscripts is not so perfect as would be necessary, if they were worthy to be placed upon the high pedestal that is prepared for them by their ardent advocates. Dean Burgon after collations extending through many years has supplied figures which it seems impossible to withstand.[2] The marks of carelessness spread over them, especially prevailing in ℵ, are incompatible with perfection. Tischendorf, after collating B, speaks of the blemishes that occur throughout.[3] Dr. Dobbin reckons 2,556 omissions in B as far as Heb. ix. 14, where it terminates.[4] Vercellone, the editor, tells of 'perpetual omissions,' 'of half a verse, a whole verse, and even of several verses.'[5] This is just what examination reveals: and ℵ is unquestionably worse. Yet doubtless in the temperate words of Dr. Scrivener, 'we accord to Cod. B at least as much weight as to any document in existence.'[6] But we cannot agree with those who rate either it or the Sinaitic extravagantly high : and the fact that these two are frequently found with a few others in a small minority must

[1] See below, Chapter VII. Canon Cook, "The Revised Version," pp. 159-183, argues this admirably. Dean Burgon thinks otherwise.

[2] "Revision Revised," p. 14, 94-5, 249, cf. 376, 384-6. My own figures, derived from a smaller collation of the five Uncials, agree mainly with those of the Dean, who says that 'the task of laboriously collecting the five "old uncials" throughout the Gospels, occupied me for five-and-a-half years, and taxed me severely.' (P. 376.)

[3] "Universa Scripturæ Vaticanæ Vitiositas."

[4] "Dublin University Magazine," 1859, p. 620. Dr. Dobbin calculates 330 in St. Matthew, 365 in St. Mark, 439 in St. Luke, 357 in St. John, 384 in the Acts, and 681 in the Epistles.

[5] Burgon's "Letters from Rome," p. 18.

[6] See "Plain Introduction," p. 116.

THEORY OF WESTCOTT AND HORT REFUTED.

make us always examine their testimony, unless it is strongly supported, with suspicion and care.[1]

[1] CHARACTER OF B.

Judged by the ordinary rules of criticism, the text of B is far from being of such a superior character as to warrant the excessive submission that Extreme Textualists claim for it. Thus, besides serious blemishes which have been already mentioned (above, pp. 27-29), we find in the face of superior readings well attested :—

(1.) Omissions of an entire verse, or of a longer passage, having all the appearance of being intrinsically genuine :—
Matt. xii. 47 ; xvi. 2, 3 (a verse and eight words) ; xviii. 11 ; xxiii. 14 ; Mark vii. 16 ; ix. 44, 46 ; xi. 26 ; Luke xvii. 36 ; xxiii. 17 ; John v. 3, 4 (a verse and five words) ; Acts xxiv. 6, 7, 8 (a verse and fourteen words); xxviii. 29 ; Rom. xv. 24.

(2.) Similar omissions of more than three words :—
Matt. v. 44 (12 words) ; xx. 16 (7) ; 22 (6) ; 23 (7) ; xxviii. 9 (7) ; Mark vi. 11 (15) ; 33 (4) ; 36 (4) ; viii. 26 (6) ; x. 7 (6) ; 24 (5) ; xi. 8 (5) ; xii. 30 (4) ; 33 (5) ; Luke i. 28 (angelic salutation, 4), iv. 4 (5) ; 5 (5) ; vi. 45 (5) ; viii. 16 (6) ; 43 (6) ; ix. 55, 56 (24); x. 22 (8) ; xi. 44 (4) ; xvii. 19 (5) ; 24 (4) ; xxii. 64 (6) ; xxiv. 1 (4) ; 42 (4) ; John i. 27 (7) ; iii. 13 (5) ; viii 59 (7) ; xiii. 32 (6) ; xvi. 16 (6) ; Acts xv. 18 (7) ; 24 (6) ; xviii. 21 (11) ; xxi. 22 (4) ; 25 (6) ; Col. iii. 6 (5) ; 1 Thess. i. 1 (8) ; Heb. ii. 7 (9) ; vii. 21 (4).

(3.) Short but important omissions :—
Matt. i. 25. αὐτῆς τὸν πρωτότοκον ; v. 22. εἰκῇ ; vi. 4, 18. ἐν τῷ φανερῷ ; xxvi. 28. καινῆς (Words of Institution) ; Mark ix. 29. καὶ νηστείᾳ ; x. 6. ὁ Θεός ; 21. ἄρας τὸν σταυρόν ; xiii. 18. ἡ φυγὴ ὑμῶν ; xiv. 22-24. φάγετε-τὸ-καινῆς (Words of Institution) ; 68. καὶ ἠλέκτωρ ἐφώνησεν ; Luke vi. 1. δευτεροπρώτῳ ; 26. οἱ πατέρες αὐτῶν ; xxiv. 53. αἰνοῦντες καί ; John vi. 51. ἣν ἐγὼ δώσω ; xiv. 4. καί . . οἴδατε ; Acts iii. 6. ἔγειραι καί ; x. 30. νηστεύων καί ; 2 Cor. v. 14. εἰ ; Eph. i. 1. ἐν Ἐφέσῳ ; 15. τὴν ἀγαπὴν τήν. Also the frequent omissions of the article, of αὐτός, of Κύριος, of ὁ Ἰησοῦς, and of similar subjects, imports an ungraceful baldness into the text. That many of these omissions, at the least, came from carelessness is shown by several passages being written twice over.—Scrivener, p. 116.

(4.) Readings inferior to those of the Traditional Text :—
Matt. xi. 16. παιδίοις . . . ἅ, κ.τ.λ. instead of agreeing participles.

The arguments therefore advanced by the School of Extreme, or as perhaps it should be called, Extravagant Textualism, break down all along the line. And we are

Matt. xv. 13. omission of τυφλῶν.
    xvi. 12. τῶν ἄρτων for τοῦ ἄρτου.
    xvii. 22. συστρεφομένων for ἀναστρεφομένων.
        23. τῇ τριημέρᾳ for τῇ τρίτῃ ἡμέρᾳ.
Mark ii. 5, 9. ἀφίενται for ἀφέωνται, i.e., his sins were not then actually forgiven!
    iii. 29. ἔνοχος αἰωνίου ἁμαρτήματος for κρίσεως.
    xvi. 4. ἀνακεκύλισται for ἀποκεκύλισται.
Luke ii. 14. ἐν ἀνθρώποις εὐδοκιάς. No rhythm and inferior sense.
    xii. 56. Clumsy repetition of οὐκ οἴδατε δοκιμάζειν for δοκιμάζετε.
    xxii. 55. περιαψάντων δὲ πῦρ for ἁψάντων.
Acts xxvii. 13. περιελόντες for περιελθόντες.
Rom. v. 1. σάρκινος for σαρκικός.
1 Cor. iii. 1. σαρκίνοις for σαρκικοῖς.
James i. 20. ἐργάζεται for κατεργάζεται.
2 Pet. ii. 12. καὶ φθαρήσονται for καταφθαρήσονται.

5. Changes obviously injurious to the sense :—

Matt. xi. 23. Too like a jeer, instead of dignified sorrow.
    xiv. 29. ἦλθεν for ἐλθεῖν. St. Peter failed in the coming.
    xxviii. 19. βαπτίσαντες for βαπτίζ.—supposing that disciples were to be made after, instead of by, Baptism.
Mark vii. 3. διὰ Σίδωνος. A geographical solecism.
Luke x. 42. ὀλίγων δὲ χρεία ἐστὶν ἢ ἑνός.
    xvi. 12. ἡμέτερον for ὑμέτερον,—a patent blunder.
Acts xxv. 13. ἀσπασάμενοι for ἀσπασόμενοι, i.e., greeted Festus first, and then went to see him!
1 Cor. xiii. 3. καυχήσωμαι for καυθήσωμαι.
1 Thess. ii. 7. νήπιοι for ἤπιοι.
Tit. ii. 5. οἰκουργοὺς ἀγαθὰς for οἰκουρούς.

(6) Changes spoiling or injuring the Grammar :—

Matt. viii. 5. εἰσελθόντος αὐτοῦ προσῆλθεν αὐτῷ.
    xv. 32. ἡμέραι for ἡμέρας. Awkward change of grammatical subject.
    39. τὸν πλοῖον.
    xxi. 19. οὐ μηκέτι γένηται.
Mark iii. 28. βλασφημίαι ὅσα ἐὰν βλαφημήσωσιν (ὅσας ἄν).

driven to seek a secure position amongst the entrenchments of the Rival School.

Mark vi. 21. θυγατρὸς ὀρχησαμένης the subject to ἤρεσεν.
    xi. 19. ὅταν ἐγένετο.
        22. ὃ ἐὰν εἴπῃ.
    xiii. 14. τὸ βδέλυγμα ... ἑστηκότα.
    xiv. 35. ἔπιπτεν for ἔπεσεν :—glaringly the wrong tense.
Luke xvii. 6. εἰ ἔχετε (for εἴχετε) ἐλέγετε ἄν.
Acts xvi. 13. οὗ ἐνομίζομεν (for ἐνομίζετο) προσευχὴ εἶναι.
    xiii. 7. τῶν Φαρισαίων καὶ (omit τῶν) Σαδδουκαίων.
Rom. v. 1. ἔχωμεν for ἔχομεν.
1 Pet. iii. 1. ἵνα κερδηθήσονται (for —σωνται). So Luke xiv. 10. ἵνα ἐρεῖ.

This list might be easily and largely increased, besides that bad spelling—to call a spade a spade—is constant in this manuscript. See Scrivener, "Plain Introduction," pp. 543-552. Burgon, "The Revision Revised," pp. 315-317, and reff. there given. Cook, "Revised Version," pp. 136-141. Michelsen, in "Theologisch Tijdschrift," Jan. 1844. See also Kuenen and Cobet, "Novum Test. ad fidem Cod. Vaticani." Leyden, 1860. Præfatio. א is admitted everywhere, except in the fond eyes of Tischendorf and of a few admirers here and there, to be greatly inferior to B.

CHAPTER V.

THE RIVAL SCHOOL.

TENETS OF THE RIVAL AND SOUND SCHOOL STATED AND CONSIDERED.

IN treating of Extreme Textualism, so much has been borrowed from the representations of the Rival School, which of late years has perhaps been chiefly known in resistance to aggressive tenets, that much less explanation of the principles maintained in it is now needful than would otherwise have been required. Nevertheless the position of the chief doctors in this School must be defined. Their attitude has been frequently and indeed strangely misrepresented. Besides which, their teaching is given, not merely in opposition or protest, but in clear and definite expression of principles.

1. And first, it must be remarked, that it is unjust to insinuate that they are set against all revision of the Greek Text. They would not be Textualists at all if they were not ready to adopt what are really the verdicts upon all the evidence. 'Again and again,' says Dean Burgon, 'we shall have to point out that the Textus Receptus needs correction.'[1] No one can read Dr. Scrivener's "Plain Introduction," a work which every clergyman should possess and study, without observing that so stiff an adhesion to the Text received from the last three centuries has no place in

[1] "The Revision Revised," p. 21, note.

his thoughts. Quotation or proof of so notorious a circumstance are absolutely unnecessary.

Nor again must it be imagined that discrimination in the employment of authorities is repudiated by them. Whilst Dr. Scrivener rejects the idea of families of manuscripts, he allows that grouping in a moderate manner is necessary in order to judge of their character and value. 'Now that theories about the formal recensions of whole classes of these documents have generally been given up as purely visionary, and the very word *families* has come into disrepute by reason of the exploded fancies it recalls, we can discern not the less clearly that certain groups of them have in common not only a general resemblance in regard to the readings they exhibit, but characteristic peculiarities attaching themselves to each group.'[1] It is inevitable that one document should have a high reputation, and another be rated deservedly low. The relative antiquity, the circumstances attending the production so far as they are known, the nature of the text so far as it reveals itself to clear and definite criticism, are admitted as demanding to be taken into account. Objection is felt to 'the glorification' of a few, so as to make them almost 'objects of superstition and idolatry:' but there the objection ceases.

2. The leading principle of the School is that all authorities should be fairly and relatively weighed. The old Uncial manuscripts according to their age and character, the later Uncials of the eighth, ninth, and tenth centuries, the Cursive manuscripts from the tenth century onwards; the Versions with reference to their antiquity and excellence; Lectionaries, as they were accredited and agreed with one another and with other manuscripts; and quotations from

---

[1] "Plain Introduction," pp. 553, 4. The italics are Dr. Scrivener's.

Fathers after their ascertained merit.[1] There is much work to be done in editing, collating, and indexing before this vast mass of evidence is ready for use. Thus these men widen the basis, and endeavour to build their superstructure upon the broadest and surest foundation. If it be objected that the work of revision is indeed formidable and must be delayed under this method of proceeding for many years, the answer is ready. It is dangerous to meddle with the Holy Scriptures, which are bound up so closely with the Faith. The changes proposed are numerous and momentous: and what if they are found to be really corruptions and depravations of the Sacred Deposit? Reverence and caution are essential in the things of God. Whatever is done must by all means be well done. A few years, or a life-time or two, long indeed in our sight, are little in the history of mankind, and still less in the eyes of Him with whom we have to do. It is better to aid humbly in a steady and wise advance than to attempt hastily to settle questions, and to end by unsettling them.

3. Such is the general system of this school of Sound or High Textualists. But in one grand point the school is at issue with the last. Extreme Textualism seems to look upon any support derived from the Traditional or Received Texts as merely supplying to readings a title to be abused and spurned,[2] instead of securing for them considerations of respect. Yet the fact, admitted several times by Drs. Westcott and Hort,[3] that the Traditional Text is fifteen hundred years old, ought surely

---

[1] For particulars, see below, Chapters VIII. IX.

[2] Any reading labelled by Dr. Hort as 'Syrian,' is summarily rejected by him with something very like ignominy.

[3] See above, p. 26, note 2.

to ensure for it other treatment. Is is probable that St. Chrysostom, the Gregories, and St. Basil, amidst an abundance of early manuscripts, with which our present stores could not be mentioned on the same day in comparison for antiquity and value, would all have been led away in the company of their great contemporaries to prefer an inferior strain of copies? Is it likely, that if they had missed the right turn, their successors in the following ages would not have discovered that they were on the wrong road, and would have failed to work back into the Royal Highway? Is it indeed possible that the great King of the new Kingdom, Who has promised to be with His subjects 'alway even unto the end of the world,' should have allowed the true text of the written laws of His Kingdom to lurk in obscurity for nearly fifteen hundred years, and a text vitiated in many important particulars to have been handed down and venerated as the genuine form of the Word of God? Could the effect of the sacred Presence of the Holy Ghost in the Church be looked for in any more important and peculiar province, than in the preservation of the fashion and lineaments of that body of written records and teaching which He Himself has inspired?

Therefore the Rival School of Sound or High Textualists is right in attributing the greatest importance to the Traditional Text, as the Text undoubtedly handed down in the Church, and importance also to the Received Text, as an excellent though by no means an exact exponent of the former of the two. This is a matter of so much moment, that the present inquiry would be far from complete, even in the limited scope which belongs to a concise guide to the main features of Textual Criticism, if it did not include a description of the salient points in the history of the Sacred Text, so far as it is known. Error usually arises from our ignoring some essential element. And the question really is, whether we ought to make a clean sweep of the past, except so much as dates of documents are concerned, and rest solely upon the uncertain glimmer of criticism formed centuries after the materials for that criticism were produced, or whether we cannot indeed discover in the course of actual events, so far as they have been made known to us, the virtual determination of this important controversy, and solid grounds of judgment which may compel and sustain a mature and sound decision.

But before entering upon a brief view of such history, one remark is needed as to the nature of the points at issue.

They depend upon an estimate of proportion,—how much value we ought to attribute to this point, and how much to that. The evidence is mainly before us, and its existence is undisputed. This indeed is the pivot upon which judgments must turn. As in sculpture, symmetry and beauty of form depend upon each limb and feature being represented in due measure, and he carries about with him the true sculptor's eye, who with readiness and precision sees where any part of the outline is enlarged or diminished or out of place; so in our decisions, whether of a pettier or a more weighty kind, the greater part of them are involved in the stress that we lay, or do not lay, upon the particulars presented to us—in fact, upon the proportion which they severally assume in our view. We may indeed err from insufficiency of evidence, or narrowness of survey: but more often our success or failure is determined by correctness or error in laying emphasis, or else by just or false discernment in the formation of our estimate.

CHAPTER VI.

HISTORY OF THE TRADITIONAL TEXT TILL THE ERA OF ST. CHRYSOSTOM.

EARLY CORRUPTION. A PURE LINE. EARLY VERSIONS. RISE WITHIN THE CHURCH OF SEMI-SCEPTICAL PHILOSOPHY, AND PRODUCTION OF A VITIATED TEXT. PROOF OF THE PREVALENCE OF THE TRADITIONAL TEXT.

COMPARATIVE Criticism must not be prosecuted in the case of the writings of the New Testament upon exactly the same principles as those which prevail in ascertaining the text of Classical Authors. It is true that generally speaking what is sound in the one case cannot be gainsaid in the other. The verdict of the manuscripts must be taken according to the principles dictated by critical acumen and established by experience. But Sacred criticism superadds some considerations of a very grave nature.

In the first place, the mass of materials of criticism is so vast, and the wealth of attested readings is so great, that there is no need of any Conjectural Emendation. The sole duty of the Textual Critic is found in assembling, weighing, and balancing the different kinds of evidence that can be brought to bear upon the passage under review. There is no demand therefore for conjecture; it is an ascertainment of facts: besides that conjecture or surmise are entirely excluded by reason of the peculiar dignity and loftiness of the subject.[1]

Secondly, the position of the Holy Scriptures as inspired by God the Holy Ghost must never be allowed to pass out of recollection. The great Inspirer of the Writings is also Himself the great Guide of the Church. Accordingly, the overruling care exercised by Him according to promise is a factor all through the history which must ever be borne in mind. Not of course that evil has been excluded from co-existing along with the good—such is the universal experience: but nevertheless the Church, as the 'Witness and Keeper of Holy Writ,' has, under His direction, cast out the evil from time to time, and has kept to a generally defined course. Serious errors might have been committed in the transmission of the works of Homer, or of Thucydides, or of Aristotle: and indeed many of the books of the last of these are supposed to have perished. But it can hardly be conceived that the Holy Ghost, after communicating His Inspiration in the composition of books, would in the midst of His overruling care have allowed those books to be varied according to changing winds of human opinion and human action, without the maintenance throughout of a form mainly at least free from error. It can scarcely be but that a succession of copies pure from any great corruption must have existed, and existed too in predominance, all down the Church's history.

Thirdly, although the separate books of the New Testa-

---

[1] See above, p. 47, note 1. Indeed, Conjectural Emendation in editing classical writings must ever be hazardous, and is not now rated nearly so high as it used to be. Dindorf's earlier text of Sophocles is much better than his later one. Successive editors usually return to the unamended text.

ment were unquestionably the productions of separate authors, and bear the traces of a distinct personality in each instance, it would be nevertheless wrong to regard them— especially the Gospels—as solely individual compositions. In their corporate, apart from their individual aspect, they were embodiments of a Teaching and Faith, which had been imparted to the Church, and taught by the Church, before those books were severally written. Immediately after the Lord's Ascension and the coming of the Holy Ghost, there came into operation a continual exercise of oral teaching, which must have gradually assumed definite system and recognised fashion and form. Since the events of our Lord's Life must have been related continually in all evangelizing action, and there must of necessity have been a large number of eager narrators, and since the subject too was one that must have enlisted all the reverence in their souls, there must also have been at work a never-ceasing corrective criticism, under which the stories told must have become, so to speak, almost stereotyped with few variations.[1] In course of time, when either the converts demanded manuals for elementary information, or Lections were needed

---

[1] The accordance in so many respects with one another of the Synoptic Gospels has been explained upon three main theories :—

(1) That the Evangelists made use of a common document, or common documents, (Eichhorn),

(2) That the later Evangelists made use of the writings of their predecessor, or predecessors, (Townson),

(3) That each Gospel was made up from a permanent type of oral teaching, (Gieseler.) See Lee on "Inspiration," Appendix L.

The last seems to me to be the best explanation, as being truest to the facts. Cf. St. Luke i. 1-4. Τῇ ἀγράφῳ τοῦ θείου κηρύγματος διδασκαλίᾳ. Euseb. "Hist. Eccl." ii. 15. Papias, τὰ παρὰ ζώσης φωνῆς, Eus. "H. E." iii. 39. Irenæus, Λουκᾶς ... τὸ ὑπ' ἐκείνου κηρυσσόμενον εὐαγγέλιον ἐν βιβλίῳ κατέθετο. Eus. "H. E." v. 8.

in the celebrations of the Holy Eucharist or in services of Common Worship, or when the want of authorized writings was felt in the studies of the faithful or in arguments with heretics, written records became requisite. The care of the Tradition and of reducing it to writing fell upon a body of men told off for the purpose under the special name of Evangelists.[1] The foundation of all was public: and it is therefore the more probable, as it is on all grounds possible, that alterations of a lesser kind might have been introduced in what may have been practically successive editions of the Holy Gospels. Besides this, in the presence of such an amount of oral teaching, which had been rendered necessary by the absence of accredited writings for some years, it could scarcely be but that in an early multiplication of copies, when those writings had been made, mistakes of various kinds would be extensively introduced, and would be very hard to expel.

Very soon, therefore, after the books of the New Testament were written, corruption began to affect them. Error

---

[1] Eph. iii. 11. Acts xxi. 8. 2 Tim iv. 5. The two functions of Evangelists, *i.e.* to preach and to have the special care of the Word (τὴν τῶν θείων εὐαγγελίων παραδιδόναι γραφήν) is declared by Eusebius, "H. E." iii. 37. St. Matthew wrote for the Hebrew Christians, St. Mark for the Church at Rome—in compliance with request (Eus. "H. E." ii. 15) —and St. Luke for the Corinthian Church. So the couplet attributed to Gregory Nazianzen—

Ματθαῖος μὲν ἔγραψεν Ἑβραίοις θαύματα Χριστοῦ,
Μάρκος δ' Ἰταλίῃ, Λουκᾶς Ἀχαιϊάδι,

I.e., for Italy and Achaia, as Ἑβραίοις shows, not as Townson takes it, *in* each of those places. St. Luke, as it appears to me, most probably wrote his Gospel during St. Paul's imprisonment at Cæsarea, when that Providential arrangement gave a pause in labour, and an excellent opportunity of collecting materials upon the spot over Judæa, Galilee, and Samaria.

has been said to have arisen from four other sources. First, there was a determined wish to alter the Holy Scriptures, so that they might witness to the heretical doctrines that were from time to time taken up.[1] Then, on the other hand, it has been asserted that the orthodox have not been free from a form of doing evil that good might come, in that they may perchance have tampered with the sacred Text, in order to convict of error assailants of the Faith. But in recent times especially, this species of error has been vastly exaggerated :[2] and as far as it did exist it was chiefly found in the middle ages, and on occasions when holiness and uprightness had descended for the moment to lower levels. Next, a great deal of debasement must be attributed to the carelessness of scribes, chiefly before the act of transcribing was brought to the perfection which it was reaching after the seventh century. And lastly, and especially in early times, ignorance of the Greek language, or of the doctrine delivered, was a fruitful cause of error.

In the first years, the scarcity of written records cannot have failed to produce much inaccuracy. And the slowness with which the true Faith on the subject became established amongst the newly converted, many of whom were Christians in name more than in anything reaching as far as sound belief, affected not only an universal acceptation of the Canonical Books, but a reception of the text of those books. Gnostic doctrines were soon found in conflict with the words

[1] αἱρετικῶν ἀνδρῶν ἀναπλάσματα. Eus. "II. E." iii. 25.
[2] Mr. Hammond ("Outlines of Textual Criticism") remarks that 'there appears no strong ground for the suggestion,' that any 'alterations for dogmatic reasons' exist. See Scrivener, "Plain Introduction," p. 18, note. This is almost a *bête noire* with some writers, who have rested it upon supposition, rather than authentic facts. See below, Chapter IX.

and composition of the New Testament. And indeed this could not have been otherwise. For Gnosticism was an attempt to combine the existing philosophy with the newly-revealed Christian Teaching. As soon therefore as Christian Doctrines were expressed in an authoritative shape, Gnosticism found itself in opposition to them. Thence arose constant attempts to mould the writings that came forth into such form and expression as would not be at variance with tenets agreeing with, or not so repugnant as Christianity to, the old philosophy and the ideas previously entertained.

The Books of the New Testament did not exist soon enough for Simon Magus, Cerinthus, and the other heresiarchs of the first period of Gnosticism, to direct their assaults upon them. But Basilides, who lived in the earlier half of the second century,[1] a native of Alexandria, the chief seat and centre of Gnosticism, rejected the Pastoral Epistles and the Epistle to the Hebrews,[2] and added other books to those which were canonically recognised.[3] After him Valentinus is said by Tertullian to have corrected the text and to have boldly maintained that readings introduced by him were older than the words generally received.[4] Marcion went much further. He divided the New Testament into two parts, 'The Gospel,' and 'The Apostolicon.' Of these, 'the Gospel was a recension of St. Luke with numerous omissions and variations from the received text. The Apostolicon contained the Epistles of St. Paul, excluding the Pastoral

---

[1] Probably about 117-138 A.D. Wordsworth, "Church History." vol. i., p. 195.
[2] See Westcott, "On the Canon," p. 296.
[3] Euseb. "H. E.," iv. 7.
[4] "De Præscriptione Hæreticorum," § 30.

Epistles and that to the Hebrews.'[1] According to Tertullian and Epiphanius, he 'mutilated and depraved' the text both of Epistles and Gospels.[2] The followers of these men, as was natural, went beyond their leaders. Nor must Tatian be omitted, a disciple of Justin Martyr, and founder of the Sect of the Encratites. His " Diatessaron," or Harmony of the Gospels, had such a circulation that Theodoret in the fifth century found in the churches of his diocese alone upwards of two hundred copies, and objected so much to the mischievous spirit in which the work had been executed, that he substituted in their room the Gospel of the Four Evangelists.[3] It is surely not wrong to trace to these influences much of the corruption which is repeatedly declared by writers about the end of the second century to have vitiated the sacred Text.

Thus Dionysius of Corinth says that he must not be surprised when people altered his writings by additions and omissions, if they tampered in like manner with the Holy Scriptures.[4] St. Irenæus tells the same story, and appears to have had the same fear.[5] Clement of Alexandria complains

---

[1] Westcott, "On the Canon," p. 314. Burgon's "Last Twelve Verses," p. 95.

[2] Westcott, p. 314. The learned Professor doubts however whether this was really true as to the Epistles. Burgon, "Last Twelve Verses," p. 94, note. Dean Burgon, " Revision Revised," pp. 34, 35, traces the mutilation of the Lord's Prayer in St. Luke by B and ℵ to Marcion.

[3] See Burgon's "Last Twelve Verses," pp. 317, 318. The Dean quotes from "Hœrct. Fab.," i., 20 (Opp. lv., 208), which I have verified. On the authority of a scholion, the Dean traces to Tatian (and Diodorus) the strange insertion by B and ℵ of the piercing of the spear into the account of St. Matt. xxvii. 49, before the record of our Lord's death.

[4] Euseb., "H. E.," iv., 23.

[5] Euseb., "H. E.," v., 20. Irenæus, "Contra Hæres," iv. 6, 1.

of people who introduce change into the Gospels.¹ An unknown writer, quoted by Eusebius, inveighs against heretics who laid hands without fear upon the Divine Scriptures, under the pretence of correcting them.² Origen speaks of the disagreement between the various manuscripts; and adds, 'But now, great in truth has become the diversity of copies, be it from the negligence of certain scribes, or from the evil daring of some who correct what is written, or from those who in correcting add or take away what they think fit.'³

And yet indications are not wanting that exceeding care was taken by the orthodox to preserve the Holy Books in their genuine and unimpaired form. Tertullian, in arguing with heretics, bids them consult the autographs of the Apostles at Corinth, or Thessalonica, or Ephesus, or Rome, where they are preserved and read in public.⁴ St. Irenæus refers in one place to 'the approved and ancient copies' for settling the number 666 in the Revelation; and in another gives most particular directions as to the careful and correct copying of a book of his own.⁵ We cannot be wrong in seeing in this latter instance, as well as in the signatures attached with extreme care to the end of the account of the

---

¹ Stromata, iv., 6. Scrivener, "Plain Introduction," p. 508 note.
² Euseb., "H. E.," v., 28. Probably Caius: Mill, "Prolegomena," p. lxii., Routh, "Reliquiæ sacræ."
³ "Comment. on Matt.," Tom. iii., p. 671, *De la Rue*, quoted by Scrivener, "Plain Introduction," p. 509. I have thought it well to give unaltered Dr. Scrivener's translation, but have verified the quotation.
⁴ "Ipsæ Authenticæ Literæ. De Præscript. Hæret.," p. 36, and Routh's Note, "Opuscula," pp. 205, 6, which Dean Burgon kindly points out.
⁵ τοῖς σπουδαίοις καὶ ἀρχαίοις ἀντιγράφοις. "Contra Hæres," v. 30, 1. Euseb., "H. E," v. 20.

Martyrdom of St. Polycarp, a reflection of the conscientious accuracy, fortified in every way, which must have directed the copying out of the best and accredited manuscripts. And the deep and loving reverence, in which the Holy Scriptures were held, is shewn later on in the severe condemnation of those who gave them up during the violent persecution under Diocletian, and in the fact that a Sect[1] arose upon the question of the amount of punishment which should be meted out to such betrayers[2] of the Sacred Books.

But the original autographs perished, and nothing has descended to us about them after the expressions employed by Tertullian.

We are, however, not left to secondary evidence for proof that the Traditional text was used and handed on in Ante-Nicene days. The witness of separate ecclesiastical writers upon controverted passages, proving that they had in their possession manuscripts agreeing with the Text afterwards adopted generally in the Church, and the renderings of the early Versions, especially the Syriac and Italic, establish satisfactorily this position, as will subsequently appear.

Early in the second century development in the spread of the Holy Scriptures was made in two directions.

That robustness of the stem of the Church which grew up at Antioch is indicated in two striking particulars recorded in the Scriptural account. The religion in that place was so genuine and characteristic, that the name was first applied there to the converts which the followers of the Lord have kept ever since. And from that city, replete with vice and degradation but the site of a structure of wondrous holiness and zeal,—preferred as the source of such evangelization

---
[1] Donatists.
[2] 'Traditores,' the technical name which was used.

before Damascus and even Jerusalem,—the great Apostle of the Gentiles was sent forth on his ever famous journeys.

In the same spirit, the Holy Scriptures were in very early times, whether at Antioch, or in Palestine, or elsewhere, translated into 'a tongue understanded of the people.' No record remains of the occasion when this translation was effected, or of the mode of action, or of the actors. The good was to be wrought, and it was done. Aramaic, or Syriac, was a more flexible language than the Hebrew. The Peshito, or 'Simple' Version has remained certainly since the sad divisions wrought in the Syrian Church during the fifth century, because the Nestorians and Monophysites, as well as the Christians of St. Thomas in India and the Maronites of Lebanon, all use it to this day, and prove therefore by such use that we must go back for its origin at least to the time when they had not separated. And it appears most probable, that it was that which was read at the first in Syria.[1] Hegesippus, in the second century, seems to speak

---

[1] Since the discovery of the Curetonian Version in Syriac by Archdeacon Tattam in 1842 and Canon Cureton, Extreme Textualists have maintained that it was older than the Peshito on these main grounds:—
1. Internal evidence proves that the Peshito cannot have been the original text.
2. The Curetonian is just such a text as may have been so, and would have demanded revision.
3. The parallels of the Latin texts which were revised in the Vulgate suggests an authoritative revision between A.D. 250 and 350.

These arguments depend upon a supposed historical parallel, and internal evidence.

The parallel upon examination turns out to be illusory:—
1. There was a definite recorded revision of the Latin Texts, but none of the Syrian. If there had been, it must have left a trace in history.
2. There was an 'infinita varietas' ("August. De Doctr. Christ.," ii.

of a Syrian translation,[1] and Melito quotes 'the Syrian' in 170[2] A.D. Ephraem of Edessa speaks of this Version as used familiarly for the national Scriptures in the fourth century.[3] The Peshito resembles the Received Text. It may have been actually in the hands of St. John.[4] It did not include all the Catholic Epistles, or the Revelation. The Peshito has been called 'The Queen of Versions.'

Soon afterwards, or about the same time, other Versions were made in the West. It was not likely that the great Latin Branch of the Church should continue long without translations of her own. There appear to have been a large number of translations made independently of one another, from the expressions used by St. Jerome and St. Augustine. 'There are almost as many standards of the text as there

> 11) of discordant Latin texts, but only one Syriac, so far as is known.
> 3. Badness in Latin Texts is just what we should expect amongst people who were poor Greek scholars, and lived at a distance. The Syrians on the contrary were close to Judea, and Greek had been known among them for centuries. It was not likely that within reach of the Apostles and almost within their lifetime a Version should be made so bad as to require to be thrown off afterwards.

As to internal evidence, the opinion of some experts is balanced by the opinion of other experts (see Abbè Martin, "Des Versions Syriennes," Fasc. 4, obligingly lent me by Dr. Scrivener). The position of the Peshito as universally received by Syrian Christians, and believed to date back to the earliest times, is not to be moved by mere conjecture, and a single copy of another Version. The Abbè Martin, after minute examination, assigns the Curetonian to the opening of seventh century.

[1] Euseb., "H. E.," iv., 22, τοῦ Συριακοῦ εὐαγγελίου.
[2] Mill, "Prolegomena," p. cxxvii, ὁ Σύρος.
[3] Scrivener, "Plain Introduction," pp. 312, 321-4.
[4] Bishop Ellicott, "On Revision," pp. 26, 27, quoted by Dean Burgon, "The Revision Revised," p. 9. The Peshito omits the 2nd Ep. of St. Peter, the 2nd and 3rd of St. John, the Epistle of Jude and the Revelation. MSS. exist from early in Cent. V.

are manuscripts,' said St. Jerome.[1] And St. Augustine speaks of 'the infinite variety of Latin translations,' and again of 'the multitude of translators.'[2] Both of those great Fathers tell of the untrustworthiness of the Versions. And no wonder. Whilst in Syria Greek was well understood, and it must have been easy there to get at the autographs themselves, or at excellent copies made directly from the autographs, in Italy, Africa, and in the other parts of the West, accurate acquaintance with Greek was comparatively rare, and the distance must have led to a large crop of mistakes. Much obscurity hangs over the old Latin Versions: but it appears probable that they included three groups, African, European, and Italian. The Italian was preferred by St. Augustine.[3]

Later than the Syrian and Latin translations, but probably dating back as far as the end of the Second Century,[4] we find the Memphitic and Thebaic Versions. Alexandria very soon became one of the most active centres of Christian teaching. Philosophy and Christianity there came into collision.

---

[1] "Prefatio ad Damasum:" 'Si enim Latinis exemplaribus fides est adhibenda, respondeant quibus : tot enim sunt exemplaria pene quot codices.'

[2] "De Doctrina Christiana," ii., 11, 15. He speaks again and again of 'diversitates interpretum,' and so forth.

[3] "Old Latin Biblical Texts," i., Introduction, p. xxx, by Professor Wordsworth, who adopts the classification of Westcott and Hort. Professor Sanday, in "Some Further Remarks on the Corbey St. James (ff.)," No. XI. of the Oxford "Studia Biblica," p. 236, which he has courteously sent me, considers that there were two fundamental main stocks, the African and the European. The f family, otherwise called Italian, the Professor supposes, after scholarly and minute analysis, to be a revision of the European. Dr. Hort too considers the Italian class to consist of Revisions.

[4] Bishop Lightfoot, in Scrivener's "Plain Introduction," p. 371.

The Memphitic, or Bahiric, sometimes but with not so much propriety called the Coptic, Version was the production of Lower Egypt. It is, speaking broadly, a fair rendering of the Greek, but generally agrees with B and ℵ and the few MSS of that class. It omits the Apocalypse.

The Thebaic or Sahidic, was the Version of Upper Egypt. This translation is generally of a character similar to the Memphitic, but having had its field away from Alexandria, does not resemble the class of MSS just mentioned so much as its neighbour does. The Apocalypse appears not to have formed part of it.

'Alexandria may be called the mother of systematic theological science.'[1] Situate near to an isthmus uniting two continents and dividing two seas, from a commanding position of unrivalled convenience it attracted to itself the literature of East and West. Greek language and art had settled down with a 'remarkable after-growth' into what was termed Alexandrinism.[2] Asia contributed much of her dreamy philosophy. The traditions of Egyptian lore had not perished. There flourished here a colony of Jews so strong and so greatly Hellenized that they required a translation for themselves of the Hebrew Scriptures into Greek.[3] And as the instance of Philo shews, they had learned to mingle a tone of Platonism with their Jewish belief.

It was not unnatural therefore that the celebrated Catechetical School should rise in such a place. Alexandria was soon known as one of the headquarters of the Early Church.

---

[1] Bishop Chr. Wordsworth, "Church History to Council of Nicæa," p. 251.

[2] See Mommsen's "History of Rome," vol. iv. pp. 575, 6.

[3] The Septuagint, from the seventy-two translators, six for each tribe.

From the time of St. Mark, said to have been the first bishop, to the middle of the second century when the school emerged into celebrity under Pantænus, Christianity was active there. And it was only to be expected, that as the philosophy of the period had in Gnosticism already simulated to some extent the form of Christianity, so it would now pursue a second course of action, and would in the next place endeavour to modify the Faith from within the Church.

Such is the probable account of the rise of Origenism; and though Origen was no Arian, yet a later offshoot of the same great stock was found in Arianism. And no one can wonder if a line of inferior texts can be traced—with a class of readings which were afterwards thrown aside in the Church—from Origen onwards till the time of the close of the Arian heresy. Debased doctrine, and readings of Holy Scripture afterwards to be rejected, would naturally go hand in hand.

The employment of corrupt manuscripts has been detected in the writings of Clement of Alexandria, the immediate predecessor of Origen in the Catechetical School, by Dean Burgon. The Dean has produced Clement's quotation of fifteen verses (Mark x. 17-31), and discovers in the 297 words of them 112 variations from the Received Text, or a discordance reaching to 38 per cent.[1] Origen must have used several copies and of various kinds.[2] Indeed, it is very questionable whether he did not execute an edition, or

---

[1] The same passage differs from Westcott and Hort's Text in 130 words, or 44 per cent. See Burgon, "The Revision Revised," pp. 326-8.

[2] Abp. Laurence. "Remarks on the Classification of MSS. adopted by Griesbach," chap. iii., iv., Appendix.

recension, of the works of the Evangelists and Apostles. It is certain that he did something like this upon the Old Testament, and there is a probability that at least to some extent he continued the same mode of treatment on to the New.[1] His authority was widely venerated and followed in later times.[2] He was a copious and precise commentator upon Holy Scripture. From numerous facts of history, he may be said to have founded a School.

Among those whom we know unfavourably at this period was Hesychius, probably an Egyptian bishop, who is said by St. Jerome to have introduced bad alterations into copies which went by his name. Another is Lucian, presbyter of Antioch, against whom the same charge is made.[3] Again, Pamphilus, bishop of Cæsarea, the great friend of Eusebius, from whom the latter took his second name (Eusebius Pamphili) and who set up the famous library at Cæsarea, copied out the works of Origen, and kept them there. He was

[1] Origen, on Matt. xix. 19. He speaks of the disagreement of the copies, ὡς πάντα τὰ κατὰ Ματθαῖον μὴ συνᾴδειν ἀλλήλοις, ὁμοίως δὲ καὶ τὰ κατὰ τὰ λοιπὰ Εὐαγγέλια. He adds that he has corrected in the Old Testament from other copies, keeping to their consentient testimony, and has put asterisks where the Hebrew did not give the expression, not liking to expunge entirely, and leaving others to adopt his reading or not, as they thought fit.

[2] Burgon, "Last Twelve Verses," p. 97; "The Revision Revised," p. 292. Cook, "The Revised Version," pp. 155-7. "Letter to Bp. of London."

[3] "Præfatio ad Damasum." See also Jerome, "Catalogus Scriptorum Ecclesiasticorum," p. 77. Cook, "Revised Version," p. 152, note. St. Jerome tells us that three editions of the Old Testament existed, viz., one of the Septuagint by Hesychius, which was followed in Egypt; another by Lucian, which was used from Antioch to Constantinople; and the third in Palestine, derived from Origen, and published by Pamphilus and Eusebius. "Præfatio in Librum Paralipomenon." Bingham, xiv. 3, 17.

said by his disciple and friend 'to have surpassed all of Eusebius' contemporaries in disinterested study of the Holy Scriptures, and in untiring and loving toil in anything that he undertook.'[1] Records of his labours undergone in conjunction with Eusebius still remain.[2] Pierius, a disciple of Origen, is also known as a diligent student of Holy Scripture,[3] and to have had, as well as Origen, copies that were called by his name.[4] He was the teacher of Pamphilus, Head of the School in Alexandria, and not wholly orthodox.[5]

So we are brought from Origen to Eusebius. And indeed, the veneration and affection entertained by the latter for the great teacher has been expressed by him frequently in his history. Cæsarea was the adopted home of the latter days of Origen. He must have spent most of his last twenty years in that city. It was his refuge after troubles in Alexandria: there he was at length ordained. His spirit must have lived on amongst his admirers: and in Eusebius of Cæsarea we see a virtual successor to his main opinions and tenets.[6]

[1] Euseb., "H. E." "De Martyr. Palæst.," p. 11. Scrivener, "Plain Introduction," pp. 512, 3.

[2] "Codex Friderico-Augustanus," subscription to Book of Ezra and Esther.

[3] Euseb., "H. E.," vii., 32.

[4] Jerome on Matt. xxiv. 36; Gal. iii. 1. See Scrivener, "Plain Introduction," p. 516.

[5] Euseb., "H. E.," vii. 32. Routh, "Reliquiæ Sacræ," iii., pp. 211-12, 265 (1814).

[6] Jerome, "Contra Rufinum," vol. i., § 8. Cook, "Revised Version," p. 168. Eusebius must have been a great student of Holy Scripture. It is to him that we owe the 'Eusebian Canons,' and as is probable also the so-called 'Ammonian Sections.' Fault being found with Tatian's "Diatessaron," because he omitted parts of the Gospels, Ammonius tried to construct a Harmony by arranging the other Gospels in parallel columns with the First, and cut them up into sections in order to bring them into parallelism with St. Matthew. The particulars of his

But during the lifetime of these men a catastrophe occurred which must have affected very greatly the transmission of the Holy Scriptures. The persecution of Diocletian and Galerius, notwithstanding the care taken and the firmness shewn even unto death, must have caused the destruction of a large number of manuscripts. Hesychius, Lucian, and Pamphilus suffered martyrdom. And after the storm passed over, there must have been a serious lack of copies of the Holy Scriptures for use in the Church, especially where the large increase of converts added to the number of congregations, and caused the building of fresh churches.

Towards the end of this long period of history, and whilst Constantine was in the midst of his Semiarian stage, he gave the celebrated order to Eusebius, probably between A.D. 330 and 340,[1] to send him fifty magnificent copies of the Holy Scriptures. They were to be written on the best vellum by skilful and accomplished penmen, and in a form

---

Sections seem to have perished: but Eusebius tells us (Epist. ad Carpianum, init.) that he himself took the hint from Ammonius, and so constructed his ten Canons, and as it appears the Ammonian Sections. He cut up the Gospels into these Sections, St. Matthew containing 355, St. Mark 233 (or more), St. Luke 342, St. John 232. The Gospels ran continuously throughout, but the Sections marked in the margin afforded a power of reference, and the Canons or Tables supplied an Index according to which the parallel Sections could be brought together. The first Canon gives 71 places in which all four Evangelists combine: the next three, where three agree, (2) Matt., Mark, Luke; (3) Matt., Luke, John; (4) Matt., Mark, John: the next five, where two coalesce; and the last supplies 251 places peculiar to some one or other of the Evangelists. A reference to the Canon was given in the margin under the number of the Section, thus: $\frac{14}{1}$. See Burgon, "Last Twelve Verses," pp. 125-132, 295-312. Scrivener, pp. 56-62.

[1] Cook, "Revised Version," p. 160.

well fitted for use. Orders were at the same time issued to the Governor of the province to supply the materials for the work, which was to be accomplished with all possible speed. Two carriages were placed at the disposal of Eusebius for conveying the copies to Constantinople, and he sent them off soon under the charge of a deacon.[1]

Now there are various reasons for supposing that B and ℵ were amongst these fifty manuscripts. They are referred by the best judges to about the period of Constantine's letter, to speak generally. In Tischendorf's opinion, which is confirmed by Dr. Scrivener,[2] the scribe of B wrote six 'conjugate leaves' of ℵ. These manuscripts are unrivalled for the beauty of their vellum and for their other grandeur, and are just what we should expect to find amongst such as would be supplied in obedience to an imperial command, and executed with the aid of imperial resources. They are also, as has been already stated, sister manuscripts, as may be inferred from their general resemblance in readings. They abound in omissions, and show marks of such carelessness as would attend an order carried out with more

---

[1] Eusebius sent them, τρισσὰ καὶ τετρασσά. "Vit. Const.," iv. 37. There are three interpretations of these words: (1) 'in triple or quadruple sheets,' in that case it would have been probably τρίπλοα καὶ τετράπλοα: (2) 'written in three or four vertical columns respectively' (Canon Cook), which would exactly describe ℵ and B, only a preposition would be wanted to turn the adjectival into an adverbial expression: (3) combined with πεντήκοντα σωμάτια ἐν διφθέραις ἐγκατασκεύοις (c. 36), 'we sent abroad the collections [of writings] in richly adorned cases, three or four in a case' (Archdeacon Palmer, quoted by Dr. Scrivener). After examining the letters, I am convinced that my friend Archdeacon Palmer is right. See Cook, "Revised Version," p. 162, 3; Scrivener, p. 513, note.

[2] Scrivener, "Plain Introduction," p. 92. "Christian Remembrancer," October, 1867.

than ordinary expedition. And even the corrector,[1] who always followed the copyist, did his work with similar carelessness to the scribe whom he was following.[2] Besides which, it is expressly stated in ℵ that it was collated with a very old manuscript corrected by Pamphilus after the Hexapla of Origen.[3] And Cæsarea was the place where manuscripts of Pamphilus and Origen would be found.

There is therefore very considerable foundation for the opinion entertained by many that these two celebrated manuscripts owe their execution to the order of Constantine, and show throughout the effects of the care of Eusebius, and the influence of Origen, whose works formed the staple of the Library of Pamphilus, in the city where they were most likely written.[4]

Such was probably the parentage, and such the production of these two celebrated manuscripts, which are the main exponents of a form of Text differing from that which has come down to us from the Era of Chrysostom, and has since that time till very recent years been recognized as mainly supreme in the Church. And the question arises, which of the two was the generally accredited Text in the period which has just passed under review.

1. Now it must first be remembered that the traces of corruption were very widely spread in the first ages of the Church. It was impossible but that oral transmission from one to another, inaccuracy and unskilfulness in writing, de-

[1] διορθώτης.
[2] Tischendorf, "Novum Testamentum Vaticanum," Prolegomena, xxiv. Cook, "Revised Version," p. 174.
[3] Subscriptions to Ezra and Esther. It is true that these are in a hand of the seventh century. Scrivener, "Plain Introd.," p. 53, note.
[4] Dean Burgon however does not agree with this conclusion, but places ℵ at least half a century after B. "Last Twelve Verses," pp. 293, 4.

fective apprehension of the Faith, and unbelief in various phases and degrees, must have given rise to a prolific progeny of error. Such indeed is the story that we hear in many quarters. But meanwhile, the amazing health and vigour of fresh Faithfulness in those early days found effect in the tree, that though hidden in part at first amidst the rank upgrowth of error shot out in course of time, and at length permanently overtopped the stunted plants that were doomed soon to decay.

2. Accordingly, in the next period we shall find the Traditional Text ere long indisputably in the ascendant. Now how could it have been thus supreme, if it had no true title? Unlawful usurpation must have been soon discovered. The fact that the supremacy was acknowledged and not gainsaid, lays a heavy burden of proof upon those who, fifteen centuries after, seek to question the right and deny the sway.

3. But there is remaining even now to us sufficient demonstration of the existence and use of the Traditional Text in the first ages. The witness borne by the early Fathers to controverted readings proves that they used Manuscripts belonging to the Traditional Class which were much older than any now in existence. Take, for example, fifteen passages which are at the present time under discussion, and the following Fathers are found to testify upon them to the Traditional readings:[1]—Ignatius (1), Papias (1), Justin Martyr (5), Irenæus (6), Tertullian (7), Theophilus of

---

[1] The passages are, Matt. i. 18; i. 25; v. 22; v. 44; xvii. 21; Mark vi. 20; xvi. 9-20; Luke ii. 14; xxii. 43, 44; xxiii. 34; xxiii. 45; xxiv. 40; John iii. 13; v. 3, 4; Acts xx. 28; 1 Tim. iii. 16. The above are almost entirely Dean Burgon's quotations. It is hard to see how any such support can be adduced for the readings of B and ℵ.

Antioch (1), Hegesippus (1), Athenagoras (1), Vincentius (1), Marcion (1), Clement of Alexandria (3), Hippolytus (6), Acta Pilati (2), Origen (11), Dionysius of Alexandria (3), Apostolical Constitutions (6), Ps. Tatian (2), Cyprian (1), Macarius Magnes (2), Julius Africanus (1), Titus of Bostra (2), Archelaus with Manes (1), Ps. Justin (1), Clementine Homilies (1), Arius (1), Eusebius (9), Athanasius (8), Aphraates the Persian (4), Didymus (10), Epiphanius (11), Ephraem Syrus (6), Ps. Ephraem (1), Gregory Nazianzen (9), Gregory of Nyssa (26), Basil (8), Cyril of Jerusalem (2), Lucifer (2), and Leontius (1). That is to say, in 165 places as relating to only 15 chance passages in Holy Scripture Ecclesiastical Writers living before the Era of St. Chrysostom are proved to have followed Manuscripts thus witnessing to the Traditional Text. It should be borne in mind that it was only at the close of this period that ℵ and B, the two oldest manuscripts now existing, were produced.

4. In a similar manner, the Peshito and Italic Versions —including under the latter class the best of the Old Latin Versions [1]—were made two hundred years before those two Manuscripts, and—especially the former—support the Traditional Text. Nor is occasional evidence subsequently wanting in the Egyptian Versions which, as has been seen, came out later in the same period.

There is therefore, as these specimens show, no warrant for asserting that the Traditional Text is not traceable back as far as the earliest age of the Church. The vestiges of it in Ante-Nicene times are of a character agreeing with its unquestionable ascendency in the future.

[1] "August. De Doctr. Christ.," ii. § 15.

CHAPTER VII.

HISTORY OF THE TRADITIONAL TEXT FROM THE ERA OF ST. CHRYSOSTOM TILL THE INVENTION OF PRINTING.

THE GREAT PATRISTIC ERA. IMPROVEMENT IN THE ART OF TRANSCRIBING. ANCIENT LIBRARIES. PARALLEL SUPPLIED BY THE LATE SETTLEMENT OF THE CANON. AGE OF MANUSCRIPTS, VERSIONS, FATHERS, AND LECTIONARIES. EVENTUAL SUPREMACY OF THE TRADITIONAL TEXT.

THE period of history that we have just surveyed in brief includes the early struggles of the Church. Though there were Christians who had received in transmission from the Apostles the Faith in its entirety and in its varied life, and had learned to realize it, and were firm in maintaining it, yet the Church had not yet come throughout her length and breadth to understand and hold it in all its proportion and detail. The work of the great men of the time 'was to construct and not to define. And thus the age was an age of research and thought, but at the same time it was an age of freedom. The fabric of Christian doctrine was not yet consolidated, though the elements which had existed at first separately were already combined. An era of speculation preceded an era of councils; for it was necessary that all the treasures of the Church should be regarded in their various aspects before they could be rightly arranged.'[1]

But the period that immediately succeeded was vastly different. The world of the time had entered at least in name into the Catholic Church. And with the disposition to half-faith which it carried along with it, and which was severely felt for at least two quarters of a century, it brought besides a sense of law and rule and order, as well as also a greater width of observation, and a desire of definition and system and of more uniformity in ritual and belief.

This period was perhaps the most remarkable of all in the history of the Church. Religious questions were the great questions of the day : the most eminent writers of the time were churchmen : and the subjects of their writings were those of the Catholic Faith. Their great object was to ascertain and unfold the exact lineaments of that which was once for all[2] delivered to the saints. The Creeds and the Canons of great Councils remain as the grand monuments of their united labour. And the works of Athanasius, Cyril of Jerusalem, Hilary, Basil, the Gregories, Ambrose, Chrysostom, Augustine, Jerome, Cyril of Alexandria, Leo the Great, and others, (if we may mention also some of those who immediately preceded this era) are as beacon-fires still shining to later ages, and telling of the greatness of the men who kindled them.

Another point in a sister field throws light upon the settlement of the Sacred Text which must have silently been effected at this time by the rejection of alien variations.

---

[1] Westcott, "On the Canon of Holy Scripture," p. 406.
[2] St. Jude, p. 3. ἅπαξ. "August. Contra Donatist.," iv. 24. 'Quod universa tenet Ecclesia nec conciliis institutum sed semper retentum est, non nisi auctoritate Apostolica traditum rectissime creditur.'

Classical literature was in the condition which always ensues when a lengthened period of production is succeeded by a time of rest. The treasures of the past are then stored, studied, and regulated. The expressions of the old writers are noted, their style is analysed, and commentators flourish in congenial soil. It is a time of dictionaries and grammars. Accordingly at this time Hesychius—a different man from the Textual editor [1]—wrote his celebrated lexicon : and the great Grammarians, Charisius, Diomedes, Donatus, and Priscian, pursued their researches and built up their system. And the stirring events of the world, under which literature was surrendered to the studious few, who as time went on worked more and more in retirement from the turmoil of life, caused this period to be long protracted, so that it was not till the eighth or ninth century that the system upon which they laboured reached the measure of perfection that it ultimately attained.

Thus with regard to punctuation. 'In the papyri of Hyperides, there are no stops at all, in the Herculaneum rolls exceeding few : Codd. Sinaiticus and Vaticanus . . . have a single point here and there on a level with the letters, and occasionally a very small break.' [2] It was not till about the seventh century, that the single point alone was used at the head, middle, and foot of letters, to indicate a full-stop, half-stop, or comma respectively. Points were afterwards multiplical (·:·. , ::) to express different powers. 'The Greek interrogation (;) first occurs in the ninth century, and (,) used as a stop a little later.' [3] In the early manu-

---

[1] Cf. Dr. Schmidt, in Smith's "Dictionary of Biography," s. v.
[2] See Scrivener, "Plain Introduction," p. 46.
[3] See Scrivener, "Plain Introduction," p. 47. "Globe Encyclopædia," s. v. Manuscripts.

scripts, there is also no separation of space between the words.

Again, Breathings do not occur in Greek Manuscripts of the Holy Scriptures till the end of the seventh century, nor indeed Accents. In the ninth century they are found, with slight exception, but not affixed with accuracy. In the seventh or eighth centuries breathings and accents were inserted in the older manuscripts, Yet they were said to have been originally invented, or more probably reduced to system, by Aristophanes, librarian at Alexandria about 240 B.C.[1]

Besides this, the spelling in the early manuscripts shewed a great defect in the art of expressing sounds by letters, and a want of recognised system in the employment of adopted methods. We find both rough variations of consonants,[2] and confusion between the several vowels and diphthongs.[3] The latter peculiarity is so common that it has earned for itself the special title of 'Itacism.' There is a tendency just at the present day amongst editors to substitute some of these ruder types of words for those which were previously received, and which are more in accordance with the orthography now accepted in Classical writings.[4] But surely this is rather to roll back the wheels of progress.

So that it would appear that the Art of Writing manuscripts did not reach anything like maturity till about the eighth century. And this is, in truth, held to be the fact. It was perfected in the Monasteries. The first care of St. Benedict

---

[1] Scrivener, "Plain Introduction," p. 44.
[2] Thus οὐθὲν for οὐδέν; σάρκινος for σαρκικῆς; Μαθθαῖον for Ματθαῖον.
[3] Thus ἔγειρε or ἔγειραι; ἴδετε or εἴδετε; ἵνα καυθήσωμαι or καυθήσομαι. Scrivener, p. 11.
[4] See "Prolegomena" to Tischendorf, 8th edition by Dr. Caspar René Gregory, pp. 71-116. Also Scrivener, "Plain Introduction," pp. 10, 12, 14.

was that there should be a library in each newly formed monastery. At Monte Cassino there was a large library which was burnt by the Saracens in the ninth century. Bobbio was famous for its palimpsests. St. Gall was also widely known. The Irish Missionaries, such as Columba, Aidan, Boniface, Kilian, were great cultivators of the art, and indeed the Irish, like the Lombards and Anglo-Saxons, had a style of their own.[1] The beautiful manuscripts, now preserved as invaluable treasures, shew the pitch of perfection to which the art was brought in later times. Manuscripts formed the field of painting: and the schools of modern painters issued originally from the bodies of artistic transcribers.

But besides the learning, study, and ability spent by the Churchmen of the era succeeding the Arian struggle, the men of that time had special advantages which have not descended to our own age. Owing to the jealous and courageous care of the Church, a large number of manuscripts must have survived the persecution of Diocletian. These must have been copied, re-copied, and copied again and again, and indeed large libraries existed in various places.

The libraries of Alexandria were especially celebrated. In the time of Ptolemy Euergetes, the library in the Bruchium contained 490,000 volumes, and that at Serapeum 40,000. The Emperor Aurelian in 273 A.D. destroyed the Bruchium, and probably one of the libraries perished at that time. But though the Serapeum was afterwards pulled down by the command of Theodosius, the libraries in that city were enlarged and increased till the troubles in connection with the Saracens ensued, and they perished in A.D. 640.

[1] Westwood, "Palæographia Sacra Pictoria." Silvestre's "Palæography," ed. Sir F. Madden.

A library was formed at Constantinople by command of Constantine, and though small at first, it must have grown at length to a great size. Burnt in 477 under the Emperor Zeno, it was again restored. And as the imperial library, it enjoyed a high reputation in the middle ages till the capture of the city by the Turks.

The library of Pamphilus at Cæsarea is said to have been increased by Eusebius to 30,000 volumes. This library also fell a victim to the Saracens. In later times, Buda under Matthæus Corvinus is reported to have possessed 50,000 manuscripts, till the city sank into the hands of the Turks in 1527, when the library was destroyed.

It seems surely clear from these considerations that we of the present time are so inferior to the Churchmen of the age of St. Chrysostom and of the succeeding ages, both in the furniture of our 'apparatus criticus' and in the knowledge of early manuscripts, that it would be rash in the extreme to overrule the verdict which they passed. And this conclusion is surely strengthened almost to demonstration, when we take into consideration the overruling care of the Holy Ghost in the Church. For the Church does not act by Councils alone, or solely in Canons or Creeds, but expresses her decisions in the universal operations of her common life. When therefore we are told, and find the information to be true as we shall see, that the text used at Constantinople and by St. Chrysostom became 'the standard New Testament of the East,'[1] and that 'the fundamental text of late extant Greek MSS. generally is beyond all question identical with the dominant Antiochian or Græco-Syrian text of the second half of the fourth century,' we find ourselves face to face with a silent action of the Church in one of her

[1] Westcott and Hort, "Introduction," p. 143; vol. i., p. 550.

grandest periods, and we cannot but yield to her virtual decision.

'Slow experience and spiritual instinct decided the practical judgment of the Church. Step by step the books which were stamped with Apostolic authority were separated from the mass of other works which contained the traditions or opinions of less authoritative teachers. Without controversy and without effort " the Gospel and the Apostles " were recognised as inspired sources of truth in the same sense as "the Law and the Prophets." In both cases the judgment appeared as the natural manifestation of the life of the Christian body, and not as a logical consequence of definite principles.'[1]

This striking description by Dr. Westcott of the settlement of the Canon of Holy Scripture is more than illustrative of the manner, in which the form of text, which now asserted itself victoriously and for ever, must have come to be generally acknowledged as supreme. The other species of readings went down before it. Practically and as far as recorded use goes, though the Codex Beza (D) was written later, the Western text vanishes. 'The most remarkable fact, standing out in striking contrast to the previous state of things, is the sudden collapse of the Western text after Eusebius.'[2] The Vatican and Sinaitic manuscripts had appeared, but writers are not found to have quoted them, and they have had in succeeding centuries so far as we know only a follower here and there, who again are left successively in rejection and solitude.

Indeed, so far does this conclusion carry us, that we are led to call in question the excessive value assigned by some

---

[1] Westcott, "On the Canon," p. 350.
[2] Westcott and Hort, "Introduction," p. 141.

Textualists to the mere antiquity of manuscripts. And taking into account the growth of the art of transcribing, and the lapse of time during the gradual expulsion of error from the text of the New Testament, we are driven to the conclusion, that the relative value of manuscripts is not determined by rude antiquity; but that a manuscript of the seventh or eighth century, or even of later production, may be superior to one of the fourth or fifth, especially if the earlier bear indications of suspicious parentage, or be produced under heretical associations. Such a manuscript though inferior to another in actual age, yet may deliver a testimony which is virtually much older : because it may witness to Traditional teachings which may be supported by evidence dating back to the earliest times. We can understand some German critics, who deeply learned as they are, have no sense of any Catholic authority[1] or of any guidance of the Church by the Holy Spirit, and who are haunted with the vision of a Church of the future constructed by pressing latent essence out of texts of Scripture and evolving hidden truths out of germs concealed within the secret consciousness of genius, which shall not have too much connection with the past, paying no attention to the silent condemnation of their theory passed by fifteen centuries. With them antiquity is valued according to its distance from now, and its nearness to the original autographs. But when the closest proximity attainable is a matter of nearer three than two centuries, and the Church of the time, with advantages with which those of the present day cannot be compared for a moment, has in

---

[1] Dr. Michelsen however, writing at Leyden, expressly rejects the extreme Textual theory because it controvenes the principle, *Quod semper, quod ubique, ab quod omnibus.* " Theologisch Tijdschrift," Jan., 1884.

tacit but consistent action pronounced upon the question, is it not difficult to see how those who acknowledge the influence of the Holy Ghost in the Church can follow such guidance, except from omission to observe the wide-spreading reach of this truth and its application to the problem before us? If such a judgment is universally accepted as valid in the case of the Canon, why has it not equal force in the determination of the Sacred Text?

The earliest fact of great importance in the history of this period was one of striking interest in the spread of the Church. In the fourth century the Goths, upon their advance from the wilds of the north to the fair south, were dwelling in Mœsia, and in one of their raids into the Roman empire carried off a Cappadocian family. Ulfilas was afterwards born amongst them, and Gothic became his native language. Brought up as a Christian, he and other Goths were forced to leave their native country by persecutions on account of their religion, and they went under the leadership of Ulfilas within the confines of the Roman Empire. He was afterwards consecrated bishop by Eusebius, and passed the first seven years of his episcopate amongst the Goths in succession to Theophilus their first bishop. The last thirty-three he spent within the borders of the Roman Empire, where he migrated again with a larger number of Goths.[1]

Finding the need of the Holy Scriptures in his native tongue, he translated into Gothic the Septuagint Version of the Old Testament and the Greek of the New. He was an Arian, but his Version is nearer to the Traditional Text than to any other. Afterwards when the Goths were in

---

[1] Max Müller, "Lectures on the Science of Language," 4th edition, pp. 188-192.

Italy, it was corrupted to some extent from Latin sources.[1]
Its date is about 360 A.D.

Towards the end of this century, or at the beginning of the fifth,[2] the great Codex Alexandrinus (A), now in the British Museum, was produced, afterwards the splendid gift of Cyril Lucas, Bishop of Alexandria, to Charles I. This great manuscript is admitted by Westcott and Hort to represent fairly the text used by the great writers of its time. It may be regarded as the oldest, and yet an independent, exponent of the Traditional Text as eventually received.[3] The divergence between A on the one side and B and ℵ on the other, if we may regard those discordant witnesses as one, is greatest in the Gospels. In the Epistles there is much more agreement between them.

At some time in the fifth century the Codex Ephraemi (C), now at Paris, was executed. It is a palimpsest written over in the twelfth century with some of the works of St. Ephraem the Syrian, according to the custom introduced from very early times on account of the scarcity of vellum.[4]

---

[1] Scrivener, "Plain Introduction," p. 405.

[2] 'I venture to maintain that the limits on both sides may be A.D. 380 and A.D. 410, and that the earlier date is more nearly correct.'—Cook, "Revised Version," p. 185. The whole chapter should be considered. Dr. Scrivener is inclined to refer A to the beginning, or else the middle of the fifth century—'certainly not much later than the end of the fourth century.'—"Plain Introduction," p. 97. Cf. Hort, "Introduction," p. 75, 'referred by the best judges to the fifth century.'

[3] 'The serious deflections of A from the "Textus Receptus," amount in all to only 842 (in 111 pages): whereas in C they amount to 1798: in B, to 2370: in ℵ, to 3392: in D, to 4697.'—Burgon, "Revision Revised," p. 14. My own figures—over a smaller area—are similar.

[4] Palimpsests were used in the days of Cicero and Catullus. Cicero, "Fam." vii. p. 18, 2; "Catullus," xxii. 5. Plutarch, "Moralia," ii. 504 D, 779 C.

The original letters were in Bentley's time so difficult to decipher, that Wetstein, to whom Bentley paid £50 to collate this manuscript, complained that it took him two hours to make out one page. The writing was renewed in 1834 by chemicals. This manuscript consists of fragments throughout the New Testament, amounting nearly to two-thirds of the whole. It lies as to character of text about midway between A and B, inclining somewhat to the latter.[1]

Various indications, occurring as if by chance here and there amidst discussions, prove that the learned men of this period were quite alive to the variations of manuscripts, and exercised critical judgment in deciding between conflicting readings. Thus St. Basil at Cæsarea, misled by his authorities as to the correct reading at the opening of the Epistle to the Ephesians, refers to the oldest of his manuscripts.[2] Again, Victor of Antioch, in the earlier half of the fifth century, tells how not finding the last twelve verses of St. Mark's Gospel in several copies, he searched amongst accurate ones, where he found it, and that he especially discovered the passage in a Palestinian exemplar of St. Mark's Gospel.[3] And Severus, at the end of the same century, describes how 'being at Constantinople he heard the passage about the piercing of our Lord's side, as supposed to be related by St. Matthew

---

[1] Scrivener, "Plain Introduction," p. 120. Dean Burgon, whilst preferring it to B and ℵ, suggests that it was used as a palimpest because it was thought to be of slight value ("Revision Revised," p. 325). It is hard to conceive such an use being made of it, if it had been rated high. It was also corrected at different times by three revisers,—another proof of want of confidence in it.

[2] Burgon, "Last Twelve Verses," p. 93. "Basil," opp. i., p. 254 E, 255 A.

[3] Burgon, "Last Twelve Verses," p. 64. Appendix E., p. 288, where the Scholion is given in full.

strenuously discussed: whereupon had been produced a splendid copy of St. Matthew's Gospel, traditionally said to have been found with the body of the Apostle Barnabas in the island of Cyprus in the time of the Emperor Zeno (A.D. 474-491); and preserved in the palace with superstitious reverence in consequence. It contained no record of the piercing of the Saviour's side.'[1] It will be observed in these instances that nothing is said about any individual opinion as to what ought to be the reading, but that the question is treated as exclusively one of authority,—what in those days when many ancient copies existed was the verdict of the oldest and best manuscripts.[2]

It will be remarked that up to the end of the fifth century we have four large manuscripts. Of these ℵ alone supplies the entire New Testament. Of A the greater part of St. Matthew has perished, that is, as far as xxv. 6, about two chapters in St. John, and about eight in the Second Epistle to the Corinthians.[3] B is perfect (except for omissions) down to Heb. ix. 14, not including the Pastoral Epistles, which were often placed after the Epistle to the Hebrews, that thus came near the middle of St. Paul's Epistles. C is full of large gaps, and, as has been already stated, contains not two-thirds of the whole. Besides these, five other frag-

---

[1] Burgon, "Last Twelve Verses," p. 315, who refers to Assemanni, "Bibl. Orient.," ii., pp. 81, 82.

[2] See also Lee "On Inspiration," Appendix G, who quotes Julius Africanus, A.D. 220 (Routh, "Rell. Sacr.," ii., p. 226), Cassiodorus, A.D. 469, "De Institutione Divinarum Literarum," Pref. ii., 538, St. Augustine (besides as already quoted), "De Consensu Evangelistarum," ii., 14, iii. 7, adding that 'similar illustrations of the critical spirit with which the Fathers conducted their critical investigations might be multiplied to any extent.'

[3] From John vi. 50 to viii. 52, and from 2 Cor. iv. 13 to xii. 6.

ments[1] are extant from the fourth and fifth centuries, of which Q is the largest, containing fragments of 235 verses from the two last Gospels.[2]

It should be remarked, that these are only the earliest according to actual discovery. It is quite within the bounds of possibility that research may bring even older manuscripts to light. The cases of ℵ and of the Codex Rossanensis (Σ), which was found at Rossano in Calabria in 1879 by Messrs. Oscar von Gebhart and Adolf Harnach, seem to point to some increase accruing to our transcriptional treasures.

It must also be remembered that some of the Versions are older than any existing manuscripts that have fallen into our hands. The Peshito probably dates[3] from early in the second century: the old Latin Versions from nearly the same antiquity: the Memphitic and Thebaic from the end of the same century: the Bashmuric, another Egyptian Version, from the next: and the Curetonian Syriac, of which the date is uncertain, must have been made before the Traditional Text was generally received, and indeed as would appear probable, about the latter end of the third or the beginning of the fourth centuries.[4] Next we come to the Gothic, a contemporary of B and ℵ, though a few years their junior. And the Vulgate meets us about A.D. 384 or 385.

In 382, Pope Damasus, in consequence of the variety of

---

[1] Viz., N^b, T and T^a, which are parts of the same MS., I¹, I², and Q.

[2] Scrivener, "Plain Introduction," p. 138. See below, Chapter VIII.

[3] See above, p. 74.

[4] I hazard the suggestion that it was made under the influence of the copies of Lucian, with which St. Jerome finds so much fault. The Curetonian shows great traces of Western corruption.

readings and the extensive corruption that prevailed in the Old Latin copies, committed the revision of them to St. Jerome. That great scholar and theologian entered upon his work, which included the Old Testament as well as the New, with great care and prudence, being anxious to make as few alterations as possible. With his Latin copies he compared some ancient Greek exemplars. He soon finished the New Testament, but his translation of the Old was not completed till the beginning of the next century, and was not considered so successful as the former. By degrees his translation won its way, and continued till the time of the Council of Trent to be the recognised Version of the Western Church. In obedience to a decree of that Council, a Revision was made under Sixtus V., but was found so faulty, that only two years afterwards the Clementine Bible was issued under Clement VIII. (1592, A.D.), and has held its place to the present day.

Besides these Versions, the New Testament was translated into Armenian in the fifth century, soon after the Council of Ephesus in A.D. 431; into Georgian about the same time;[1] and also into Ethiopian at a date which is so uncertain that this Version has been assigned by Dillman to the fourth century, and by Gildemeister and other Orientalists to the sixth or seventh.[2]

In the sixth century the Cambridge Manuscript Codex Bezæ (D) was produced. It contains the Gospels and the chief part of the Acts but with several omissions, and is one of those which are called 'bilingual' manuscripts, that is,

---

[1] Dr. Malan ("Select Readings," p. 18), shews this from the standard "History of Georgia," published at St. Petersburg in 1849, and other authorities.

[2] Scrivener, "Plain Introduction," p. 409.

containing both a Greek and a Latin version. It is supposed to represent the Western Text, and is extremely inaccurate and full of interpolations. It is said to have six hundred bold and extensive interpolations in the Acts alone.[1] Its place in St. Paul's Epistles is considered to be filled by the Codex Claromontanus, so called from having been found at Clermont (D. of St. Paul), but as far as the Greek version is concerned, much more correct than its sister.

To this time also is referred the Codex Rossanensis (Σ), which contains the whole of St. Matthew, and St. Mark down to xvi. 14, and is remarkable as the earliest MS. that gives the doxology for the Lord's Prayer in St. Matthew.[2] Also the Codex Laudianus (E of the Acts), now in the Bodleian library, and various fragments, amongst which are the palimpsest Z at Dublin, and others.

The seventh century does not appear to be rich in the production of extant copies, unless it be at the end. But in the eighth, ninth, and tenth they not only abound, but with the exception of L, Ξ of St. Luke, and Δ in St. Mark,[3] witness to a now settled agreement in the Traditional Text. Perhaps the most noticeable amongst them is the Codex Basiliensis (E) now at Basle, which is usually referred to the eighth century, but is considered by Dean Burgon to belong to the seventh.[4]

In the tenth century, cursive writing came into vogue, and

---

[1] Scrivener, p. 126.

[2] But the Doxology has much earlier authority in the Peshito and Thebaic, not to mention the Curetonian, in the Liturgies, and in the Apostolic Constitutions, and the Teaching of the Apostles. See Malan, "Select Readings," p. 26. And below, Appendix v.

[3] Westcott and Hort, "Introduction," p. 171.

[4] Scrivener, "Plain Introduction," p. 127. Burgon, "Guardian" newspaper, Jan. 29, 1873. See below, Chapter VIII.

was used thenceforwards down to the time when copying gave way to printing. No less than 1997 cursive copies are now known to exist in all kinds, that is, inclusive of Gospels, Acts and Catholic Epistles, St. Paul, Apocalypse, and Lectionaries of the Gospels and of the Apostles.[1] With hardly any exception the Cursives witness to the Traditional Text. Only a few, such as 1, 33,[2] as well as 13, 69, 124, 346, and a very few others here and there, follow B and ℵ. Thus it would appear that the text of those Uncials was advocated by a small minority, and that it was nevertheless condemned, not because it was not known, but on account of its faulty nature.

The question naturally arises, What is the value of the Cursive Manuscripts? They were produced so many centuries after the Apostles' time, that serious doubts have been entertained about their possessing any critical value at all.

Now a moderate application of the principle of Genealogy here comes into action. The Cursive Manuscripts were the representatives, not only of a long line of ancestors, but as must follow from the circumstances attending them, of a long line of respectable ancestors, whose character as revealed in their extant descendants proves them not to have degenerated—speaking generally of them in the mass—in any very considerable degree, unless it be in a few particulars. Their overwhelming number supplies a presumption, and indeed more than a presumption, that their ancestors were also numerous. And their general agreement amongst themselves proves that they express the settled conviction of the Church of their time, whilst their consonance with the mass of the

---

[1] Scrivener, "Plain Introduction," p. xxx.
[2] Only 1 and 33 are quoted by Westcott and Hort, "Introduction," p. 171.

Uncials that went before them demonstrates their unbroken unison with the ages that lately preceded them.

But to dream of arraying the Cursives as a body on the one side against the Uncials as an army on the other would be abhorrent to Textual Criticism, and such a notion could only be suggested or imputed by those who are innocent of the facts of the case as well as of the principles accepted by Textual Critics. The Cursive Manuscripts, be it never forgotten, follow the main body of the Uncials with a very remarkable unanimity. Always excepting some half-dozen—those just mentioned—they bear generally the same witness. As exponents of the Traditional Text, they acquiesce in the lead of the elder testimony which is supplied by Uncial Manuscripts, Versions, and Fathers, and add confirmation to what is otherwise attested. As well suppose that the rank and file of the English Army may be drawn up against the officers, as imagine a general conflict between the Cursives and the Uncials. It should be remembered, though too much stress must not be laid upon this truth, that in the age of the Cursives the Art of Transcribing reached its highest point of perfection.

It would not be right to leave this long period from the Era of St. Chrysostom, even in a short sketch like the present, without lingering for a moment upon a very important and peculiar class of Manuscripts. Of the Lectionaries the number discovered and catalogued has now mounted up to more than five hundred. These manuscripts date back at least as far as the eighth century, and represent a tradition much earlier than that.

Lectionaries have evidently a peculiar value because of their use in Public Worship, where they would be subjected necessarily to continual criticism. Faults would be corrected, and a general accuracy ensured; though no doubt such errors as might happen to creep in would keep an obstinate hold when once in possession.

As to Versions, there are two in Syriac to be noticed since the beginning of the sixth century, and some of an unscientific order. That called the Jerusalem, of which only one manuscript exists, dates back certainly as far as the sixth and perhaps to the fifth century. A more important version was the Philoxenian, or Harclean. This was made by Polycarp, a Rural-Bishop (χωρεπίσκοπος), for Xenaias or Philoxenus, Monophysite Bishop of Mabug, or Hierapolis, in A.D. 508. About a hundred years after (A.D. 616) it was revised by Thomas of Harkel. 'It is probably the most servile version of Scripture ever made.'[1] The other Versions are :—the Slavonic, of the ninth century; the Anglo-Saxon, from the eighth to the eleventh; a Frankish of the ninth; two Persic, of the Gospels only, and of uncertain date; and some Arabic translations of small critical value.

The witness of the Fathers in the early part of this period has been stated to be consentient, and to be consistently in favour of the Traditional Text. It has been calculated that there are about a hundred Fathers who wrote before the production of B, and about two hundred more till the end of the sixth century.

We have now reached the era when printing was applied to the New Testament, and when therefore the periods cease during which materials were manufactured for the subsequent use of Textual Criticism.

A few words in retrospect are here necessary.

The great feature in this period was the rise of the Traditional Text into a predominance which was scarcely dis-

[1] Scrivener, "Plain Introduction," p. 328.

puted. Corruption of a manifold kind had been infused in the earliest times into the Sacred Writings. When they were hardly emerging from the rude depravation to which they were subjected in many places, they experienced the influence of a School of Semi-sceptical philosophy within the Church, and a small Class of copies varying from the Text afterwards accepted was produced in the times, if not as it appears under the supervision, of a party that was not wholly orthodox. Then ensued an era when the Faith of the Church and the Holy Scriptures were subjected to long and anxious consideration. The main features of the Faith once delivered were defined in Creeds. No special enactments embodying formal definition were made upon the Canon or the Text of the Holy Scriptures. Nevertheless the number of genuine Books, and the true Form of Text, were settled quietly and yet decisively. Divergent tongues were scarcely heard afterwards except to be silenced. The 'still small Voice' was making Itself felt and acknowledged throughout the whole Body, without rising into loud tones of command, or causing laws to be written down in special or general legislation.

CHAPTER VIII.

MATERIALS OF CRITICISM.

I. MANUSCRIPTS (*a*) UNCIAL, (*b*) CURSIVE; II. LECTIONARIES AND LITURGIES; III. VERSIONS; IV. ECCLESIASTICAL WRITERS.

THE research of modern times has collected, as has been already seen, a vast amount of varied evidence upon the Text of the New Testament. We may best arrange their evidence under four Heads, viz., Manuscripts Uncial and Cursive, Lectionaries and Liturgies, Versions, and the Quotations that are found in Ecclesiastical Writers.

I. (*a*) UNCIAL MANUSCRIPTS.

The New Testament was formerly divided into four parts, viz., Gospels, Acts and Catholic Epistles, Pauline Epistles, and the Apocalypse.

Uncial Manuscripts were originally made up of continuous writing in large letters without any space between the words or sentences. The most ancient letters were upright and square: afterwards they became narrow, or oblong, or leaning; and the writing gradually assumed a more elaborate and artistic form. The copies of the New Testament that have descended to us are not written upon the reed papyrus, or on wax tablets, or the bark of trees, or any such perishable substance, but generally on either vellum or the skins of very young calves, or else on parchment or the skins of sheep and goats. The Sinaitic is made up of the skins of antelopes.

The dates in the following Table (see pp. 108, 109) are taken from Dr. Scrivener's "Plain Introduction," with the exception of E, with respect to which I have followed Dean Burgon, who has carefully examined that manuscript.

Besides the Uncial Manuscripts which are mentioned in the Table, there are several smaller fragments, which with the others make up the following number in all:—

Gospels	61
Acts and Catholic Epistles	14
Pauline Epistles	22
Apocalypse	5
	102

But in this calculation, as will be observed, inasmuch as the number of authorities in each class is given, those Manuscripts which include parts of more than one class are reckoned under each. Thus A and ℵ are reckoned in all four classes, B in three, and D in two. Subtracting these, viz., 7 repetitions in the Acts, 8 in St. Paul, and 4 in the Apocalypse, we have a general total of 83 Uncials.

(b) Cursive Manuscripts.

The vast amount of Manuscripts included in this important class,—important because of their number, of their general consentience in rendering, of the strong body of ancestors which they represent, of the perfection of the art with which they were executed, and of the generally accepted conclusions of which they are the signs and tokens,—with the one weighty drawback of defect in antiquity—prevents any possibility of a list of them being given in a small work like the present. The most celebrated are the handful of dissentients that follow B and ℵ (see above, p. 101), which have been thereby lifted into a prominence beyond their real importance, and the following :—

13. Regius, collated by Professor W. H. Ferrar.
20. Regius, 188.
61. Codex Montfortianus (above, p. 9).
66. Codex Galei Londinensis.
69. Codex Leicestriensis.
71. Lambeth, 528.
113. Codex Harleianus, 1810, Brit. Mus.
124. Cæsar-Vindobon. Nessel. 188, Lambec. 31.
237—259. Collated by C. F. Matthæi.
507—517. Collated by Dr. Scrivener.
603. &c. &c. &c.

Dr. Scrivener and Dean Burgon have raised the number of known Cursives to—

Gospels	739
Acts and Catholic Epistles	261
Pauline Epistles	338
Apocalypse	122
	1460.

It is improbable, that a list has been yet obtained of all the surviving treasures of this Class. Yet on the other hand, it is scarcely conceivable, that any future discoveries will affect their general testimony to the Traditional Text.

TABLE OF CHIEF UNCIAL MANUSCRIPTS.

Cent.	Name.	Place.		Gospels.	Acts and Catholic Epistles.		Pauline Epistles.		Apocalypse.
IV.	Vaticanus	Vatican.	B	All.	All.	—	As far as Heb. ix. 14.	—	—
	Sinaiticus	St. Petersburg	ℵ	All.	All.	—	All.	—	All.
V.	Alexandrinus	Brit. Museum	A	From Matt. xxv. 6. Omit John vi. 50—viii. 52.	All.	—	Omit 2 Cor. iv. 13—xii. 6.	—	All.
	Ephraemi	Paris	C	Fragments = about ⅔ of whole.	About ⅔ of whole.	—	About ⅗.	—	About ⅗.
	Guelpherbytanus B	Wolfenbüttel	Q	235 Verses of St. Luke and St. John.					
VI.	Rossanensis	Rossano	Σ	As far as Mark xvi. 14.					
	Beza	Cambridge	D₁	All with hiatus ...	All with hiatus.	—			
	Claromontanus	Paris					All except Rom. i. 1-7, 27-30.	D₂	
	Coislin, 202	Paris and St. Petersburg.					12 leaves.	H₂	
	Guelpherbytanus A	Wolfenbüttel	P	486 verses of All Evangelists.					
	Dublinensis	Dublin	Z	290 verses of St. Matthew.					
	Nitriensis	Brit. Museum	R	516 verses of St. Luke.					
	Purpurens	Brit. Museum, Rome and Vienna	N	12 leaves and 33 at Patmos.					
	Laudianus	Bodleian			Acts i. 1—xxvi. 29; xxviii. 26—end.	E₂			
	Coislin I. (Septuag. Octateuch)	Paris, &c.	Fa	9 verses.	7 verses.	—	10 verses.	—	
VII.	Basiliensis	Basle	E₁	All, except Luke iii. 4-15; xxiv. 47-53.					

Cent.	Name	Location	Sym.	Contents	Sym.	Contents	Sym.	Contents
VIII.	Regius	Paris	L	All, except Matt. iv. 22—v. 14; xxviii. 17-20. Mark x. 16-30; xv. 2-20. John xxi. 15-25.				
	Mosquensis	Moscow	V	All, except Matt. v. 44—vi. 12; ix. 18—x. 1; xxii. 14—xxiii. 35. John xxi. 12-25; After John vii. 39, in Cursives.				
	Barberini	Rome	Y	John xvi. 3—xix. 41.				
	Zacynthius	Bible Society	Ξ	Luke i. 1—xi. 33.				
	Vaticanus, 2066	Vatican					B_2	All.
IX.	Wolfi B	Hamburgh	H	Fragments.	H_2	Acts, except 4 places.		
	Cyprius	Paris	K	All.	K_2	Cath. Ep. only.		
	Augiensis	Cambridge					F_2	Defective in 4 places.
	Boreeli	Utrecht	F_1	Full of hiatus.				
	Mutinensis	Modena			—	All Luke, Mark except 105 verses, 531 of the rest.	—	All, except 2 places.
	Tischendorfianus IV.	Bodleian	Γ					
	Mosquensis, 98.	Moscow						
	Sangallensis	St. Gall	Δ	All, except John xix. 17-35.			G_3	Defective in 6 places. Down to Heb. xiii. 10.
	Boernerianus	Dresden						
	Angelicus	Rome			L_2	From Acts viii. 10.		
	Petropolitanus	St. Petersburg	Π	All, except Matt. iii. 12—iv. 18; xix. 12—xx. 3; John viii. 6-39.				
	Porphyrianus	St. Petersburg			P_2	All, except 3 places.	—	All, except 8 places.
	Campianus	Paris	M	All.				
	Monacensis	Munich	X	With serious defects.				All, except 3 places.
X.	Nanianus I	Venice	U	All.				
	Vaticanus, 354	Vatican	S	All.				
	Harleianus	Brit. Museum	G	Fragments.				

א is quoted thus:—א*, the original reading; אa, the first corrector (IVth cent. Tisch., VI. Scrivener); אb, second c. (VI.); אc (VII.), and eight others.
B:—B*, original reading; B² or B³ first and second Diorthota; B³ first corrector (X. or XI.).
C:—C*, or ¹, first corrector (VI.); C**, or ², second (IX.); C***, or ⁴, third.
D:—corrected, first, by the original penman as Diorthota; afterwards by eight or nine others, some nearly coæval with the Codex, some not very long ago. suppl. (IX.) filled up some omissions—Scrivener, Plain Int, Tischendorf, Prolegomena (C. R. Gregory).

II. LECTIONARIES AND LITURGIES.

The value of this class of evidence, the full force of which was first advocated and explained by Dean Burgon in his 'Last Twelve Verses of St. Mark's Gospel,'[1] is very considerable and peculiar.

It is evident that what is constantly read under authority in public must have a far greater weight than the writings of any individual author. Such texts must have been continually exposed to general criticism. Whilst therefore it is quite possible that some of the MSS. that have descended to us may not have been subjected to such searching examination, and indeed that in the natural wear and tear of time the best accredited may have been most used and therefore have soonest perished, whilst those that were least in repute may have been preserved because of general neglect, Lectionaries and Liturgies emerge from the full light and the never-ceasing life of the Early Church. Add to this, that both these species of evidence date from the earliest times. The Lectionary-system of the 'Unchangeable East' has remained from very ancient antiquity, and can be traced back beyond B and ℵ to the times at least of Origen and even Clemens Alexandrinus at the end of the second century. The Manuscripts go back as far as the eighth century: but numerous indications in the works of Ecclesiastical writers carry the reference without doubt to the period just mentioned.[2]

This Lectionary-system was drawn upon the main lines of the practice that previously prevailed in the Synagogues of

[1] Pp. 191-211, 214-5, 217-24, 240, 313-5, 318.
[2] Burgon, "Last Twelve Verses," pp. 191-211.

the Jews. There were in their Services, as in ours, two Lessons, one from each of their great divisions of the Old Testament. St. Paul and St. Barnabas found at Antioch in Pisidia the ordinary custom in operation of reading both from the Law and the Prophets.[1] This habit was continued in the Liturgies by the selections then made both from the Epistles and Gospels, and in the daily Morning and Evening Prayers by the Lessons from the Old and New Testaments. Accordingly, Justin Martyr, writing about A.D. 150, records in his Apology that there were readings during Divine Service from the Apostles and the Prophets.[2] The new Lectionary-system was thus, as well as in other particulars,[3] grounded upon the old. And thus Lectionaries, as well as Liturgies, constitute a most valuable source of true information and evidence.

Several errors may be traced to this influence. Thus the omission of the last twelve verses of St. Mark's Gospel in certain copies, of which B and ℵ are the only extant specimens, is probably due to the fact that those verses constituted by themselves a Lection, which exactly filling the last page of the Gospel (for St. Mark stood last according to the Western arrangement) dropped off perforce with the last leaf. A copyist, charged to transcribe a copy so mutilated, not unnaturally mistook the end ($\tau\acute{\epsilon}\lambda o\varsigma$) marking the close of the previous Lection for the end of the entire Gospel. Again, the two verses in St. Luke that describe the ministering Angel and the agony and bloody sweat[4] were omitted in the ordinary reading of the rest of the passage on the Tues-

---

[1] Acts xiii. 15.
[2] "Apol.," i. p. 67. Burgon, "Last Twelve Verses," p. 193 note.
[3] E. g., both began in September. Burgon, p. 193.
[4] Luke xxii. 43, 44.

day after Sexagesima, and were inserted after St. Matt. xxvi. 39 on Maundy Thursday. As marks were put in the Evangelistaria directing the omission, it was even obvious that some copyist would be sure to leave the two verses out altogether. So again, the fourteenth chapter of St. John is made to commence with the words, 'And Jesus said unto his disciples,' as any one may see by referring to the Gospels in our Prayer-Book for St. Philip and St. James' day.[1] Similar introductions and insertions were not uncommon, and have crept into the Uncial Manuscripts.[2]

Lectionaries were of two kinds :—

1. Evangelistaria, or Evangeliaria, consisting of Lessons from the Gospels. Of these 415 Manuscripts are known.

2. Praxapostoli or Apostoli, containing Lessons from the Acts and Epistles, and amounting to 128, as hitherto reckoned.

The value of the Quotations in Liturgies rests upon much the same foundation as the verdicts of the Lectionaries. They 'record the witness, not of individuals, but of Churches.' But the quotations are rare. Such however is the rendering of the 'Gloria in Excelsis' in the Liturgy of St. Clement and in that of St. James. Such again is the general witness in favour of the Doxology as a recognized termination of the Lord's Prayer.

The Liturgies reach at least as far back as the 4th or 5th Centuries.[3]

---

[1] Compare the Gospels for the second, third, and fourth Sundays after Easter.
[2] See Burgon's "Last Twelve Verses," chapter xi., for numerous instances of this kind.
[4] Daniel, "Codex Liturgicus," Tom. iv., Prolegom., pp. 28-31.

III. Versions.

The chief Versions have been already noticed. The general dates of them all may be seen together in the following Table:—

Cent.	Syriac.	Latin.	Egyptian.	Single Versions.
II.	Peshito (1)	Old Latin (1) sc. a. African b. European	. . . . . ? Memphitic, or Bahiric (2) ? Thebaic, or Sahidic (2)	. . . .
III.	. . . . .	. . . . .	? Memphitic and Thebaic . . . . . Bashmuric, or Elearchian (3)	. . . .
IV.	? Curetonian (3)	Vulgate (2)	. . . . .	. . . . Gothic (2)
V.	Jerusalem (3) Karkaphensian (3)			Armenian (2) Georgian (3) Ethiopian (2)?
VI.	Philoxenian (3) A.D. 508.			
VII.	Harclean (3) A.D. 616.			
		Clementine Revision A.D. 1592.		Slavonic (3) IXth. Anglo-Saxon (4) VIIIth-XIth. Frankish (4) IXth. Persic (4) IXth. Arabic (several) VIIIth, &c.

The figures here attached to the names of the several Versions denote their relative scale of excellence in a critical light according as Dr. Scrivener has classed them. Some of the Arabic, and one Persic Version, may be ranked in the third class. But the other Persic (and perhaps one Arabic) version being derived from the Peshito Syriac, and the Anglo-Saxon or old English from the Latin Vulgate, can be applied only to the correction of their respective primary translations.[1]

The value of this kind of evidence is patent upon an inspection of the Table above. Versions present the most ancient form of continuous text. Some of them are of much earlier date than the oldest Uncials. But to this lofty position some drawbacks are attached.

1. The exact reading of a Version may perhaps be very difficult to ascertain. Questions as to the true form of the text may come into them as they do into the original Greek Text. Old Latin affords an instance before all others,[2] since it is rather a Group of Versions, African, European, and Italian,[3] than a single Translation like the rest that can be

---

[1] "Plain Introduction," p. 309.

[2] "Old Latin Biblical Texts," i., by Professor Wordsworth, Introduction, p. xxx. The chief Texts for Jerome's Vulgate, which Professor, soon to be Bishop, Wordsworth is engaged in editing, are

           Codex Amiatinus, about A.D. 541.   am.
next,   ,,   Fuldensis   VIth. .   .   fuld. or fu.
perhaps, ,,   Forojuliensis VIth. .   .   for.

[3] Of these Professor Sanday considers the Italian to be a Revision of the European. See also, pp. 75, 76. Dr. Hort's classification is—

I. African, *e, k,* &c.

II. European, *a, c, ff, h, i,* &c.

III. Italian, *f, g,* &c.

"Introduction," pp. 78-84. Wordsworth, p. xxx.

But no certain conclusions have been reached on this point.

determined with more or less accuracy. Thirty-eight codices exist, out of which the highest in repute are:—

	Century.	Letter.
Cod. Vercellensis	IV.	a.
„ Veronensis	IV. or V.	b.
„ Colbertinus	XI.	c.
„ Palatinus	IV. or V.	e.
„ Brixianus	VI.	f.
„ Corbeiensis (2)	VIII.	ff 1.
„ Sangermanensis (2)	IX.	g 1.
„ Claromontanus	IV. or V.	h.
„ Vindobonensis	V. or VI.	i.
„ Bobbiensis	IV. or V.	k.
„ Mai's Speculum	VI. or VII.	m.
„ Monacensis	VI.	q.

This drawback is not so great in the case of the others, but subtracts from the value of all.

2. From the nature of Translations, which, to be good, must adhere to the idiomatic expression of the language into which they are made, it follows that great uncertainty must prevail as to the original Greek words. Versions, therefore, do not always render decisive evidence upon the question of a single Greek expression. On the other hand, the authority of a Version as to the authenticity of a clause, sentence, or longer passage, is unquestionable, and may be much higher than that of a single manuscript, since it has presumably a public character, varying however according to circumstances, and may have a much higher antiquity.

3. It is evident that only a master of the language can at first hand pronounce upon the Version.

IV. ECCLESIASTICAL WRITERS.

Ecclesiastical writers may be said to surpass even Versions in reaching back to early, or rather the earliest Antiquity. Their authority, especially in confirmation of what is attested by good evidence of other kinds, is often of the highest importance. Their variety and number, as representing various parts and epochs of the Church, add greatly to their weight. And the positions, opportunities, and abilities of very many amongst them render their witness nearly always entitled to respectful attention. But some points subtract from their authority in this province.

Their testimony is seldom continuous, but fragmentary, and sometimes not to be had when we most need it. They often quote loosely as if from memory. Sometimes they cite from the copy that they happen to have at the moment, and so the same passage is found in different forms at different places in their writings.

But for all this, they furnish a most valuable kind of evidence. It is not necessary to attribute to them severally any critical acumen, though there is reason for inferring that more of this was to be found in earlier times than many people suppose. Their chief value is as witnesses to facts. Their evidence may be described as that of Manuscripts at second hand, of which the greater part are either older than, or about as old as, the oldest Manuscripts in existence. They often confirm readings by witnessing to the copies used by them with (so far) unquestionable accuracy. Indeed, this has been the most neglected and undervalued help to criticism, and nevertheless promises to be one of the most important. Unfortunately, their works want to be edited with this view and indexed, before all the treasures that lie hid at present are ready to the hand of Textual Critics. When that is done, supplies will have been provided for a fresh and real advance.

Such is the vast field that must thoroughly be explored before a Revision of the Greek Text can be satisfactorily accomplished. Trust must not be reposed in one class of evidence alone. Even Manuscripts of the Greek Testament, superior as they are in most respects to all the other classes, can by no means support a claim to the highest antiquity. Single Manuscripts are actually surpassed in this respect by Versions[1] and Fathers, and virtually also by Lectionaries and Liturgies.

---

[1] It should be observed, with reference to the age of the Peshito, that MSS. of it exist as far back as to A.D. 411, the date of Cod. Add. 12150, which is nearly also the date of A. See "An Account of a Syriac Biblical MS.," &c., No. viii. in the Oxford "Studia Biblica," by the Rev. G. H. Gwilliam, who has courteously sent me a copy.

CHAPTER IX.

PRINCIPLES OF CRITICISM.

(1) THE TRADITIONAL TEXT, (2) EXTERNAL EVIDENCE, (3) THE SEVEN CANONS OF INTERNAL EVIDENCE. CONCLUSION.

AS the chief parts of the province of the Textual Criticism of the New Testament have now been reviewed, we are in a position to arrive at definite conclusions with respect to the principles that ought to guide us in the revision of the Sacred Text.

And first, there can be no sort of question that it would be culpably wrong to throw aside any portions of the existing evidence. Besides the illogical nature of a process that would take no note of materials that must have weight in constructing the premises and determining the conclusion:—to go no further than the formidable project of extirpating the vast mass of multiform proof both known and increasing of a Text other than the one which it is sought in some quarters to establish, and a very questionable attempt to get rid of inconvenient testimony:—the Church is answerable before Almighty God for making due use, and for the preservation from generation to generation, of the materials collected for the maintenance of His Inspired Word. If it be replied that it is not possible for any one age to deal with so large an amount of matter, the answer is ready that it is our duty in such a case, where we are dealing, not with human circumstances but with the things of God, to reverse the poets' maxim, and to say

> *Non* mihi res, *sed* me rebus subjungere conor.

We cannot carve for ourselves the witness of the Sacred Word, but we must conform our dealings to what we find existing. Far better is it to linger in wise and reverent caution, than perhaps to rush in where angels might fear to enter, and to pull down with hasty profanity instead of strengthening the pillars of the Temple. The Great Giver of the Inspired Word is also the Preserver of it in the witness and keeping of Holy Writ. He has spoken during all the the ages, though in the still gentle Voice that He is pleased to use, yet by definite and manifest signs and tokens. We must gather these together as far as we are able, and whilst we shrink from refusing to hear their testimony, and from prejudicing or forcing their decision, we must dutifully and practically collect their verdict.

I. It will therefore follow that the first object of a Textual Critic should be to discover what is in deed and in fact THE TRADITIONAL TEXT. How far does the Received Text accord with it? For with the Text as now 'Received' operations must be begun. The burden of proof lies with alterations. Then, in what particulars has human infirmity vitiated in any one age, period, or epoch, that pure Text which may become clear to the view upon a comparison of all the ages? In the assemblage of the entire body the errors of any individual may be made manifest. General Councils used to correct the mistakes of single bishops.[1] The Holy Ghost does not eliminate all weakness, but He

---

[1] See especially, "Concilium Hispalense (A. D. 619), Mansi," x. p. 558. Canon VI.

guides the awards of the whole Church. Any Father, or Version, or even Lectionary, or copy, however ancient, however likely on all grounds to have escaped blundering, may yet have gone astray. But in the union of them all, and in testimony varied, multiplied, and mainly consentient, there is not only the proverbial strength, but there is also the promised Presence, that descended after the Lord left the earth, and is immanent in the Church onwards to the end.

II. Hence secondly, all Testimony should be mustered, and due importance assigned to every item in it. The more variety of converging evidence there is found, the more perfectly that all provinces in the Church, and all periods—especially the oldest of them—concur in attestation, so much the greater is the weight. The sources of decision will be discovered in the classes described in the last chapter. There is never (speaking practically) a lack of sufficient evidence: and the conclusions will follow which, whether from intrinsic importance, or from variety, or from number, are found after wise, enlightened, and discriminating examination to be in the ascendant.

III. Internal evidence of either kind is a long way inferior to external proof, on which the authenticity of passages will be established, but it is useful in its place. Such are the Seven Canons, viz.;

1. The harder the reading, the less likely is it to have been invented, and the more likely to be genuine. 'Proclivi lectioni præstat ardua' (Bengel). Thus δευτεροπρώτῳ, 'second first,' in St. Luke vi. 1, could hardly have been coined.

2. The more concise reading is better than the more diffuse. 'Brevior lectio præferenda est verbosiori' (Griesbach). So St. Luke xii. 56, 'Ye hypocrites, ye know how to interpret

the face of the earth and the heaven : but how is it that ye know not how to interpret this time?'¹ The second 'ye know not how to interpret' (οὐκ οἴδατε δοκιμάζειν) spoils the simplicity of the text.

3. That reading is preferable, which will explain the origin of the variation (Tischendorf). Thus Melita (Μελιτὴ) for Melitene (Acts xxviii. 1), as has been before explained.²

4. The reading which is characteristic of the author is the more probable. Great caution should be exercised in applying this canon, as such varying estimates are formed of authors' styles. But it affords strong confirmation of the authenticity of the celebrated section of the adulteress ('Pericope adulteræ') since the style of the passage (John vii. 53, viii. 11) is just that of St. John.

5. The special genius and usage of each authority must be taken into account in estimating the weight that it ought to bear. Accordingly we must always suspect the omissions of B, the carelessness of א, and the interpolations of D.

6. 'Apparent probabilities of erroneous transcription, permutation of letters, italicism and so forth,' will naturally be taken into account. So ἑτέροις (Matt. xi. 16) is evidently for ἑταίροις : and the readings 'Titius' or 'Titus Justus' have plainly arisen from a reiteration of letters.³

7. Whatever makes nonsense, or injures the meaning or construction, is probably not the true reading.⁴ For example,

---
¹ "Revised Version." Contrast the neatness of the Authorized.
² Above, p. 28, note 3.
³ Above, p. 29, note 1.
⁵ The seventh usually given is Griesbach's, viz., that suspicion must ever rest upon such readings as make especially for orthodoxy. Archbishop Magee and Dr. Scrivener have fully disproved the soundness of this imputation cast by sceptics upon the orthodox. "Plain Introduction," pp. 497-9. See above, p. 69, and note 2. The canon which I have

'the last' (ὁ ἔσχατος) in St. Matt. xxi. 31, the reading of D, making the son who went not to be the obedient son, cannot have been the true production of the Evangelist.

But all these considerations must be wisely dealt with, and kept in their place. Exaggeration in the estimate of any one of them may lead to false deduction, and authority, as declared in external evidence, must mainly decide all questions.

The true Guide in all is GOD the Holy Ghost, Who, reverently sought in purity of heart, humility of soul, and wisdom of mind, will in His Own due time and after His Own perfect counsels lead the Church and Her children to ascertain with sureness, from clear and decisive evidence, the real Form and Outline of that Sacred Word Which He Himself taught His servants by His Holy Inspiration to deliver.

May He so receive and direct all our study of His Divine Sayings through the Lord JESUS CHRIST!

placed in the text surely carries its own recommendation. Whatever human element is found in the Inspired Word of God (see Lee on "Inspiration"), nonsense or solecism have no place there. It would be well if more weight were always attributed in Sacred Textual Criticism to sound sense. The best critics employ it with manly strength. For instances, see above, pp. 27-29, and p. 57, note 1.

APPENDIX.

APPENDIX.

AN examination of a few important passages is here appended, which may serve to illustrate the controversy now existing, and to exhibit in their operation the principles already explained.

The evidence adduced is mainly derived from the eighth edition of Tischendorf's "Novum Testamentum Græce," Dr. Scrivener's "Plain Introduction," Dean Burgon's "The Revision Revised" and "The Last Twelve Verses of St. Mark," Canon Cook's "Revised Version of the First Three Gospels," and Drs. Westcott and Hort's "The New Testament in Greek."

I. THE LAST TWELVE VERSES OF ST. MARK'S GOSPEL.

A. Against their authenticity, as alleged :—
  1. ℵB. L inserts a short and manifestly spurious conclusion before the Twelve Verses.
  2. No Cursives. A few follow L.
  3. One Old Latin MS. (k), two Armenian MSS; two Æthiopic, and an Arabic Lectionary.
  4. Eusebius, Jerome, and Severus of Antioch, are also quoted. These verses are said to be omitted in the Ammonian Sections.
  5. (a) About twenty-one words and phrases, not found in the rest of St. Mark, are said to occur in these verses, as $\pi o \rho \epsilon \acute{u} o \mu a \iota$, $\tau o \hat{\iota} \varsigma$ $\mu \epsilon \tau'$ $a \dot{u} \tau o \hat{u}$ $\gamma \epsilon \nu o \mu \acute{\epsilon} \nu o \iota \varsigma$, $\theta \epsilon \acute{a} o \mu a \iota$, $\mu \epsilon \tau \grave{a}$ $\tau a \hat{u} \tau a$.

  (b). The description of Mary Magdalene, $\dot{a} \phi'$ $\mathring{\eta} \varsigma$ $\dot{\epsilon} \kappa \beta \epsilon \beta \acute{\eta} \kappa \epsilon \iota$ $\dot{\epsilon} \pi \tau \grave{a}$ $\delta a \iota \mu \acute{o} \nu \iota a$, is said to be a sign of the introduction of a new passage not containing what had gone before, where she has been recently mentioned.

(c). The note of time πρωϊ πρώτῃ σαββάτου is thought to be needless, and out of place.

B. For :—
1. All other Uncials, *i.e.* ACDEFGHKMSUVXTΔΠΣ :— also L.
2. All Cursives.
3. (a) Peshito, Harclean, Jerusalem, and Curetonian Syriac.
   (b) All Old Latin except k, and Vulgate.
   (c) Memphitic, and Thebaic.
   (d) Gothic, Æthiopic (except two MSS), Georgian, Armenian (except two MSS.), Arabic.
4. All Lectionaries. This passage was read everywhere during the Season of Easter and on Ascension Day.
5. Fathers :—
   Cent. II. Papias, Irenæus, Justin Martyr, Tertullian.
   ,, III. Hippolytus, Vincentius at 7th Council of Carthage, Acta Pilati.
   ,, IV. Syriac Table of Canons, Eusebius, Macarius Magnes, Aphraates, Didymus, Syriac Acts of the Apostles, Epiphanius, Leontius, Pseudo-Ephraem, Ambrose, Chrysostom, Jerome, Augustine.
   ,, V. Leo, Nestorius, Cyril of Alexandria, Victor of Antioch, Patricius, Marius Mercator.
   ,, VI. and VIII. Hesychius, Gregentius, Prosper, John (Abp. of Thessalonica), Modestus (Bp. of Jerusalem).

REMARKS.

B leaves a whole blank column—'the only blank one in the whole volume'—*i.e.*, of the New Testament, as well as the rest of the one containing v. 8, thus showing that a passage was left out. Either ℵ was here simply copied from B, a supposition probable on other grounds, and confirmed by Tischendorf's and Scrivener's opinion that the Scribe of B wrote this part of ℵ, in which case we have merely B over again, but without its mute confession of error; or they both followed here the common archetype from which they were confessedly derived. Eusebius elsewhere witnesses for the verses, and here only mentions loosely that some copies omit them. Jerome and Severus only copy Eusebius' expressions.

The alleged internal evidence has been demonstrated to be visionary,—a mere mistake : and is accordingly no longer urged by the critics.

Besides all this, the cause of the omission by careless or incompetent scribes is evident. The error of B and ℵ was clearly derived from a copy of St. Mark, which had lost its last leaf. A mark stood here in the Western copies of the Gospel. It is further not improbable that some scribe mistook the 'End' of the Lection, Τέλος, for the End of the Gospel, and a few others followed him. The error was ere long discovered.

This evidence plainly leaves no sort of doubt. No Court of Law could decide against the verses. It is difficult to see how it can be otherwise than discreditable to Textual Science, that the question should be held in some quarters to lie still open.

II. The First Word from the Cross.

(St. Luke xxiii. 34.)

A. Against their authenticity :—
   1. ℵ^a (first corrector), B, D* (first reading).
   2. 38, 82, 435.
   3. Two or three MSS. of Italic (a, b, d ?), Thebaic, two MSS. of Memphitic.
   4. Arethas.

B. For :—
   1. ℵ* $^{and\ c}$ (first reading and third corrector), ACD $^{gr.\ 2}$ (second corrector), FGHKLMQSUVΓΔΛΠ. E puts an * ; —these are all the other Uncials.
   2. All other Cursives.
   3. All other Versions, including the Syrian, and the other Italic and Memphitic MSS.

4. Ecclesiastical Writers :—
Cent. II. Hegesippus, Irenæus.
„ III. Hippolytus, Origen, Apostolic Constitutions, Clementine Homilies, ps.-Tatian, Archelaus' disputation with Manes.
„ IV. Eusebius, Athanasius, Gregory of Nyssa, Theodorus of Heraclea, Basil, Chrysostom, Ephraem Syrus, ps.-Ephraem, ps.-Dionysius Areopagita, Acta Pilati, Syriac Acts of the Apostles, Ps.-Ignatius, ps.-Justin.
„ V. Theodoret, Cyril, Eutherius.
„ VI. Anastasius Sinaita, Hesychius.
„ VII. Antiochus Monachus, Maximus, Andreas Creticus.
„ VIII. John Damascene, ps.-Chrysostom, ps.-Amphilochius, Opus Imperfectum.

Besides Latin Writers, such as Ambrose, Hilary, Jerome, Augustine, &c., &c.

6. This would be a most unlikely interpolation in all ways. The internal evidence is also admitted (Hort, 68) to make eminently for the genuineness of the passage.

Evidence is clearly not evidence, if any doubts about the authencity of this passage remain. The errors of a few scribes, in the face of the notorious depravation of the Sacred Text in early times, are no foundation for doubt.

III. THE RECORD OF THE STRENGTHENING ANGEL, THE AGONY, AND THE BLOODY SWEAT.

(St. Luke xxii. 43, 44.)

A. Against :—
1. ABRT. In Γ the verses are obelized, and they are marked with asterisks in ESVΔΠ.
2. None (see below). Obelized in five, and asterisks in five. A scholion in 34 says that the verses are omitted in some copies.

3. Most Memphitic codices, some Thebaic, some Armenian, and f of Old Latin. Some Armenian insert v. 43.
4. Hilary and Jerome say that some Greek and Latin MSS. omit the passage. Athanasius and Cyril of Alexandria did not mention it when they might. John Damascene in one passage omits it.

For :—
1. ℵ¹DFGHKLMQUXL. Also ESVΔΠ and Γ (see above).
2. All Cursives. But 13, 69, 124, 346, insert the verses after St. Matt. xxvi. 39, instead of in St. Luke. 13 inserts v. 43 in the right place.
3. Peshito, Curetonian, Harclean, Jerusalem, Ethiopic, some Thebaic, some Memphitic, some Armenian, all but one Old Latin, and the Vulgate.[2]
4. They are thus transferred in all Evangelistaria, the reason being that they were ordered to be read with the passage in St. Matthew on Maundy Thursday, and to be omitted on the Tuesday after Sexagesima.
5. Cent. II. Justin, Irenæus.
   „ III. Hippolytus, Dionysius of Alexandria, ps. Tatian.
   „ IV. Arius, Eusebius, Athanasius, Ephraem Syrus, Didymus, Gregory Nazianzen, Epiphanius, Chrysostom, ps. Dionysius Areopagita.
   „ V. Julian the Heretic, Theodorus of Mopsuestia, Nestorius, Cyril of Alexandria, Paulus of Emesa, Gennadius, Theodoret, Oriental Bishops in Council, Ps. Cæsarius, Theodosius of Alexandria, John Damascene, Maximus, Theodorus the Heretic, Leontinus of Byzantium, Anastasius Sinaita, Photius ; besides the Latins,—Hilary, Jerome, Augustine, Cassian, Paulinus, Facundus; —*i.e.* in all 'upwards of forty famous personages from every part of ancient Christendom.'[3]

---

[1] Scrivener, "Plain Introduction," p. 599, note.
[2] Malan, "Select Readings," p. 26.
[3] Burgon, "Revision Revised," pp. 80, 81. These lists of the

6. The verses bear every trace of genuineness. Even Dr. Hort admits (p. 67) that 'it would be impossible to regard these verses as a product of the inventiveness of scribes.'

The omission by some scribes, and the obela and asterisks inserted by others—evidently as guides in reading—are satisfactorily explained by the Lectionary usage of omitting the verses in St. Luke, and reading them with the parallel passage in St. Matthew. Even A inserts the mark of the Ammonian Section, and thereby confesses the omission. In the face of so much evidence, it is impossible that any doubt at all should remain.

IV. THE ANGELIC HYMN.

ἐν ἀνθρώποις εὐδοκίας

for

ἐν ἀνθρώποις εὐδοκία.

(St. Luke ii. 14.)

A. For the alteration :—
1. ℵ* AB* D.
2. No Cursives.
3. Old Latin, Vulgate, and Gothic.
4. Irenæus (but see below), Origen (see however below), Hilary, and the Latin Fathers.
5. Mozarabic and Ambrosian Liturgies.

B. Against :—
1. ℵ^c B³ EGHKLMPSUVΓΔΛΞ, *i.e.* all the rest.
2. All Cursives.
3. Peshito, Harclean, Jerusalem, Memphitic, Ethiopic, Georgian, Armenian, Slavonic, Arabic.[1]
4. Cent. II. Irenæus.
 „ III. Origen (3), Apostolic Constitutions (2).
 „ IV. Eusebius (2), Aphraates (2), Titus of Bostra

Ancient Writers are extracted from the work of the learned Dean, who gives the references in every case.

[1] Malan, "Select Texts," p. 49.

(2), Didymus (3), Gregory Nazianzen, Cyril of Jerusalem, Epiphanius (2), Gregory of Nyssa (4), Ephraem Syrus, Philo of Carpasus, Chrysostom (9), an Antiochian.

Cent. V. Cyril of Alexandria (14), Theodoret (4), Theodotus of Ancyra (5), Proclus, Paulus of Emesa, Council of Ephesus, Basil of Selencia.

„ VI., VII., VIII.—13 testimonies.[1]

5. The Liturgies of St. James and St. Clement, and the Morning Hymn attached to the Psalms in A.

6. The rhythm of the hymn would be destroyed, since it consists of three parallel and contrasted members, making up one stanza.

This evidence speaks for itself. The opposed reading is a Western one, which was just strong enough to make itself felt in the East, as the witness of A shows, but got no further. The only consistent MS. evidence for it is found in the Western D.

V. THE DOXOLOGY IN THE LORD'S PRAYER.

(St. Matt. vi. 13.)

A. Against the Passage :—

1. ℵBDZ.
2. 1, 17, 118, 130, 209. Some scholia exist to the effect that these words are omitted in some copies.
3. Nearly all the Old Latin MSS., Vulgate, most Memphitic, Persian of Wheelocke.
4. Mozarabic, Ambrosian, and other Latin Liturgies.
5. The silence of the following Fathers :—
    Tertullian (De Orat. 8).
    Cyprian (De Orat. Dom. 27).
    Origen (De Orat. 18).
    Augustine (Epist. Class. iii. 12).
        (De Serm. D. in Monte).
        (Serm. 56-59).
        (Enchiridion, 115, 116).

[1] Burgon, " Revision Revised," pp. 420, 1.

Cyril of Jerusalem (Cat. xxiii.) (Myst. 5, 18.)
Maximus (Expos. Orat. Dom.)
Gregory of Nyssa (De Orat. Dom., v. end) may be said to be doubtful.

6. It is held that the Doxology was probably introduced, as some writers confessedly quote it, from the Greek Liturgies, where too it was separated by the 'Embolismus,' or intercalated paraphrase on 'Deliver us from Evil,' from the last petition in the Lord's Prayer.

B. For :—
1. ΣEGKLMSUVΔΠ. [ACPΓ are deficient here].
2. All other Cursives, even 33, which usually sides with אB.
3. Peshito, Old Latin, (k, f, g^1, q), Thebaic, Curetonian, Harclean, Jerusalem, Ethiopic, Armenian, Gothic, Georgian, Slavonic, Erpenius' Arabic, Persian of Tawos.[1]
4. Greek Liturgies. The 'Embolismus' was confessedly *intercalated* between integral parts of the Lord's Prayer, as a paraphrase of a petition. The following have the doxology, though with occasional variations, St. James, St. Peter, St. John, St. Mark, St. Clement, St. Dionysius, St. Ignatius, St. Julius, St. Eustathius, St. Chrysostom, St. Marutha, St. Cyril of Philoxenus, Philoxenus of Hierapolis, Dioscorus, James Baradatus, Matthæus Pastor, James (bp. of Botna), James of Edessa, Moses Bar-Cepha, Philoxenus (bp. of Bagdad), &c., &c.[2]
5. Fathers : Διδαχή, 31 (Bryennius) with variation.
    Apostolical Constitutions (iii. 18) (vii. 25 with variation.)
    Ambrose (De Sacr. vi. 5. 24.[3])
    Cæsarius (Dial. I. 29.[4])

---

[1] Malan, "Select Readings," p. 26 ; "Seven Chapters," pp. 57, 86-92 ; Scrivener, "Plain Introduction," pp. 571-3.

[2] Renaudot, "Liturg. Or.," vol. ii. ; Malan, "Select Readings," p. 26.

[3] St. Ambrose, in "De Sacra.," v. 4, professedly quotes St. Luke.

[4] Cf. In "S. Greg. Libr. Sacram. Notæ, Migne, Bibl Petr. Lat." 78, p. 291.

Chrysostom (In Orat. Dom.) (Hom. in Matt. xix. 13.)
Opus Imperfectum (Hom. in Matt. xiv.)
Isidore of Pelusium (Ep. iv. 24.)
Theophylact (in Matt vi. 13.)
Euthymius Zigabenus (in Matt. xi. 13.) (Contra Massalianos, Anath. 7.[1])

6. (a). Under any circumstances, with two Forms, there must have been many omissions by writers who followed the shorter Form. Those who dispute the authenticity of the Doxology as part of the Lord's Prayer, have not only to prove the use of the Prayer without the Doxology, but must also disprove the existence of the Doxology as an integral member of the Prayer ;—the omission of it not only by St. Luke, but by St. Matthew also.

(b). The admitted omission of the Doxology in St. Luke, and the fact that the Lord's Prayer in its other Form is complete without the Doxology would satisfactorily account for its being left out by some scribes also in St. Matthew, besides that this might have arisen solely from the intercalation of the Embolismus.

The evidence is too strong and too ancient, reaching back unintermittedly to the second century, as in the Peshito, the Διδαχή, some Old Latin, and the Thebaic, to allow hesitation in receiving the Doxology as an authentic part of the Lord's Prayer, and of St. Matthew's Gospel. The omission is due to a Western reading, of a similar character to the last, though somewhat more strongly supported.

VI. THE SON OF GOD'S ETERNAL EXISTENCE IN HEAVEN.

Ὁ Ὢν ἐν τῷ Οὐρανῷ.
(St. John iii. 13.)

A. Against the genuineness of the words :—
1. ℵBLT[b]. ὤν is omitted by A.*
2. 33.

---

[1] Wrongly quoted by Tischendorf on the other side.

3. Ὅν is omitted by Evangelistarium 44.
4. Ethiopic (?), one MS. of the Memphitic.
5. Armenian versions of Ephraem's Tatian, Eusebius (2) (?), Cyril of Alexandria (?), Origen (?).

B. For :—
1. AEGHKMSUVΓΔΛΠ. CDF fail us here.
2. All Cursives, except 33.
3. All Evangelistaria.
4. Peshito, Curetonian, Harclean, Jerusalem, Old Latin, Vulgate, Memphitic (except one MS.), Ethiopic (?), Georgian, Armenian.
5. Origen (2), Hippolytus, Athanasius, Didymus, Aphraates, Basil, Epiphanius, Nonnus, ps. Dionysius Alex., Eustathius, Chrysostom (4), Theodoret (4), Cyril of Alexandria (4), Paulus of Emesa, Theodorus of Mopsuestia, John Damascene (3), Ambrose, Hilary, Jerome, Augustine, and eighteen others, &c.[1]
6. The hardness of the words renders it impossible for them to have been invented.

This evidence precludes all doubt.

VII. God Manifested in the Flesh.

(1 Tim. iii. 16.)

There are three readings, viz., $\overline{\Theta S}$ (*i.e.* Θεός), ῝ΟΣ, and ῝Ο.

A. Evidence for ῝ΟΣ, as claimed :—
1. ℵ* A* (?) C* (?) F? G?
2. 17, 73, 181?
3. Apostolus 12, 85, 86.
4. Gothic, Peshito? Memphitic? Thebaic? Armenian? Ethiopic? Arabic of Erpenius?
5. Cyril of Alexandria? Epiphanius? Theodorus of Mopsuestia?

B. Evidence for ῝Ο, as claimed :—
1. D* of St. Paul (Claromontanus).

[1] Burgon, "Revision Revised," p. 133.

APPENDIX.

2. No Cursives.
3. Old Latin, Vulgate, Peshito? Memphitic? Thebaic? Æthiopic? Armenian?
4. Gelasius of Cyzicus, and an Unknown Writer (App. to Chrysostom).

C. Evidence claimed for Θεός ($\overline{\Theta S}$):—
1. A? KLP.
2. 260 Cursives, *i.e.* all except two.
3. 36 copies of the Apostolus.
4. Harclean, Georgian, Slavonic.
5. Cent. III. Dionysius of Alexandria.
  „ IV. Didymus, Gregory Nazianzen, Diodorus of Tarsus, Gregory of Nyssa (22 times), Chrysostom (3), a Book Περὶ θείας σαρκώσεως.
  „ V. Cyril of Alexandria (2), Theodoret of Cyrus (4) an anonymous author, Euthalius, Macedonius.
  „ VI. Severus of Antioch.
  , VIII. &c. John Damascene, Epiphanius of Catana Theodorus Studita, some Scholia, Œcumenius, Theophylact, Euthymius.

REMARKS.

(I) Evidence for ″Ος :—
1. The question whether A witnesses for ″Ος or for $\overline{\Theta S}$ must depend upon the answer to the prior question whether the two cross lines were originally there or not. Now Patrick Young, Huish, Bp. Pearson, Bp. Fell, Mill, Bentley, John Creyk, Berriman, Bengel, Woide in 1765, say that the reading was $\overline{\Theta S}$. On the other hand, Griesbach, in 1785, and since that time Davidson, Tregelles, Dr. Westcott, Dr. Hort, and Bp. Ellicott,—Dr. Scrivener in 1860 dissents—pronounce against the lines. But
  (a) Berriman added, 'If therefore at any time hereafter the old line' (*i.e.* inside the Θ) 'should become alto-
  'gether undiscoverable, there never will be just cause
  'to doubt but that the genuine and original heading
  'of the MS. was $\overline{\Theta S}$.'

(b) Woide in 1785 declared that he could not see the lines which he had actually seen in 1765.

(c) Any one may convince himself by inspection that the MS. is too far gone to admit of any trustworthy opinion being now formed, and as is probable in many a past year.

There can be no real doubt, therefore, that A did witness for θεός. The adverse testimonies have been given since Woide spoke; and indeed Griesbach said in 1785 that curious fingers had then rendered any certain conclusion impossible.

2. As to C, Wetstein, Griesbach, and Tischendorf on one side are balanced by Woide, Mill, Weber, and Parquoi, on the other. A palimpsest is a most unsuitable witness in such a delicate question. C must be held to be neutral.

3. Both F and G, which are admitted to be copies of the same MS.,[1] have here a straight line *above* the two letters slightly inclining upwards. The question is, whether it be the aspirate, in which case they would witness for Ὅς, or the sign of contraction, as for θεός. The arguments appeared to be balanced. F and G must therefore be set aside as neutral.

4. Cursive '181' cannot be found.

5. The Peshito, Memphitic, Thebaic, and Ethiopic Versions, probably witness to Ὅ.

6. The Armenian and Arabic are indeterminate.

(II.) The evidence for Ὅ is admitted not to be very strong. Such as it is, it is against both of the other readings and cannot be held to be confirmatory of either.

(III.) The comparison of Ὅς with θεός remains :—

1. 'Proclivi lectioni præstat ardua.' Ὅς is the harder grammatically, but θεός is decidedly the harder if the sense is consulted, since there could hardly be a more audacious change than to foist this word wrongly into the text.

---

[1] See above, p. 47, note 3.

APPENDIX.   137

2. Ὅς is likely to be a degeneration from $\overline{\Theta S}$: but not $\overline{\Theta S}$ from Ὅς.
3. When admitted, Θεός explains μυστήριον, and makes better grammar.
4. But the burden of decision must, as always, rest upon the evidence. Now
    a. There is no strong leaning either way of Uncials or Versions, though the inclination of Uncials is towards Θεός.
    b. The very remarkable unanimity of the Cursives indicates a practical decision of the Church before manuscripts had reached their most perfect condition, *i.e.* in Uncial times.
    c. The overwhelming testimony of Fathers to MSS. in their use, reaching back further than any existing MSS., adds a very powerful witness.

On the whole, the evidence decidedly shows that Θεός is genuine.

INDEX.

[*For Alexandrian MS., Vatican MS., &c., and A, B, &c., see under Codex; and for Peshito, Vulgate, &c., see under Versions.*]

	PAGE
ABBOT, professor Ezra	23
Accents	89
Acta Pilati	85
Acts and Catholic Epistles	101, 106, 107
Agony and Bloody Sweat	2, 111, 128-30
Aidan, St.	90
Alexander II., the emperor	24
Alexandria, 77-8, 70, 89—	
libraries at	90
Alexandrian readings	51
Alexandrian text (so-called)	41, 51
Alter	17
Ambrose, St.	87
Ammonian Sections	80 note 6
Angelic Hymn, the	130-1
Angelic Salutation	57
Anglo-Saxon Scribes	90
Antioch	51, 73
Apocalypse	101, 106, 107
Apostoli	112
Apostolical Constitutions	85, 100 note 2
Aphraates	85
Archilaus with Manes	85
Arianism	78, &c.
Ariminum, Council of	52
Aristophanes	88
Arius	85
Athanasius, St.	85, 87
Athenagoras	85
Athos, Mt.	17
Augustine, St.	75, 87
Aurelian	90
Authorized Version, from what text	12
Autographs, the	72, 93
Barnabas, St., 97—his epistle	46
Basil, St.	63, 85, 87, 97
Basilides	70
Beezebul	28
Benedict, St.	89
Bengel	15, 16
Bentley	14-15, 21, 31, 50, 96
Beza	10-11, 12
Bilingual manuscripts	11, 99
Birch	17
Boniface	90

INDEX.

	PAGE
Breathings	88
British and Foreign Bible Society	22
Bruchium	90
Buda	91

Burgon, Dean, his works, 33—misrepresented, 30 — principles, 34—great Patristic knowledge, 53 note. Also 31, 46, 47 notes 1 and 2, 52 note, 56, 60, 71 note, 78, 100, 106, 107, 110, 117

Buttmann, Philip 20

Cæsarea	83
Caius	71
Canon of Holy Scripture	104
Catholic Antiquity	93
Ceriani	36
Cerinthus	70
Charisius	88

Childhood of Textual Criticism 12-19

Chrysostom, St., 17, 35, 63, 83 87, 102—age of . . . 86-91

Church, the, silent action of, 91—duty of . . . 118-19

Clement of Alexandria 41, 71, 77

Clementine Homilies . . . 85

Cobet 35

Codex—see also Manuscripts.
A (Alexandrinus) presented by Cyril Lucar, 13—when produced and character, 95. Also 16, 21, 26, 33, 35, 50, 97, 106
B (Vaticanus) when produced, 81-3—character, 54-9—blunders, 26-29

Codex—see also Manuscripts —(*continued*).
—how estimated, 43-4, 27, 34, 35, 46, 56. Also 9, 15, 21, 36, 39, 40, 48 &c., 88, 92, 95, 97, 101, 103, 106, 107, 110
א (Sinaiticus) how found, 24-5—when produced, 81-3— character, 54-9 — carelessness, 53 — how estimated, 26, 34, 35, 46. Also 26, 36, 39, 40, 48 &c., 88, 92, 95, 97, 101, 106, 107, 110
C (Ephraemi, Parisian) date, 95-6—character, 96 . . . Also 21, 26, 97
D (Bezæ, or Cambridge), date, 99 — character, 100 . Also 11, 41, 92, 106
D of St. Paul (Claromontanus) 11, 100
E (Basiliensis) . . 100, 106
E of the Acts (Laudianus) 100
F of St. Paul (Augiensis) 32, 47 note 3.
L (Regius), 23 note 1, 49 note 1, 100
Δ (Sangallensis) in St. Mark 100
Ξ (Zacynthius) . . 22, 100
Σ (Rossanensis) 48 note, 98, 100
Friderico-Augustanus . 24
Montfortianus (61) . 9, 107
See also Table, 108, 109, and 21 note 1, 22, 49

INDEX.

Codex—see also Manuscripts
—(*continued*).
  note 1, 98, 100, and
  Uncial Manuscripts, and
  Cursive Manuscripts.
Columba 90
Complutensian Polyglott, 7-8, 10, 12
Conjectural Emendation . 65-6, 47
    note 1
Constantine . . . 81-3, 55, 90
Constantinople, library at . 91
Cook, Canon, 34-5, 27, 31, 51
    note, 56 note
Cornelius' servants 28
Courcelles, or Curcellæus . 13
Corruption of Text, causes
  and extent of 68-72
Cry, Our Lord's last . . . 2
Cure in pool of Bethesda . . 2
Cursive Manuscripts, 106-7—
  number of, 100-1—value of,
  101-2—follow the Uncials,
  102 . . . Also 16, 18, 22, 61
Cyprian, St. 21, 85
Cyril of Alexandria, St. . . 87
Cyril of Jerusalem, St. . . 85, 87
Cyril Lucar 13

Damasus 98
Dancing-girl 27
Davidson, Dr. 19
Diatessaron, Tatian's . . . 71
Διδαχή . . . . 100 note 2
Didymus 85
Diocletian, persecution of, 48, 73, 90
Diomedes 88
Dionysius of Alexandria . 41, 85
Dionysius of Corinth . . . 71
Dobbin, Dr. 55

Donatus 88
Doxology in the Lord's Prayer,
    131-3, 100, 112
Eclipse of the sun 3, 46
Edessa 51
Elzevir, Abraham 11
—— Bonaventure 11
Encratites 71
Ephraem, St. 85
—— Ps. 85
Epiphanius 71, 85
Erasmus 8-10, 12
Eucharist, Holy 68
Eusebian Canons . . 80 note 6
Eusebius . 79-83, 22, 23, 35, 41,
    55, 71, 85, 91
Evangelistaria, or Evangeliaria, 112
Evangelists . . . 68 and note
Evidence, External . 61-2, 32, 34,
    118, 120
—— Internal, place of, 45-6,
  120—seven canons, 120-22.
  Also 39, 54
Extreme Textualism . . 20-30

Families of MSS. (so-called),
    40-1, 50-1, 16, 17, 18, 61
Fathers, 116-7—their value,
  116—Manuscripts at second
  hand, 116—older than any
  existing MSS., 117—not
  uncritical, 96-7 — mainly
  support the Traditional
  Text, 91, 103 . Also 7, 16, 21,
    22, 34, 62, 73
Fell, bp. 13
Ferrar, Professor W. H. . . 107
Fredcric Augustus 24
Froben 8

INDEX.

	PAGE
Gebhart, Oscar von	98
Genealogy	40, 47-9, 101
Ghost, GOD the Holy	66, 119, 122
Gloria in Excelsis	112, 130-1
Gnosticism	70, 78
GOD manifested in The Flesh	134-7
Golgoth	28

Gospels, Synoptic, whence rose their accordance, 67 note— why written, 68 note — number of MSS. of . 106, 107

Gregory, Dr. C. R.	11 note, 23
—— Nazianzen, St.,	63, 68 note, 85, 87
—— of Nyssa, St.	63, 85, 87
Griesbach	17, 18
Gutenberg	7
Gwilliam, Rev. G. H.	115 note

Harkel, Thomas of	103
Harnach, Adolph	98
Hegesippus	85
Hesychius	79, 81
—— the Lexicographer	88
Hilary, St.	21, 87
Hippolytus	85
Hort, Professor,	25-30, 35, 38-59, 76 note 3, 114 note 3
Hugo, Cardinal	10
Hyperides	88

Ignatius, St.	84
Inscription on the Cross	3
Infancy of Textual Criticism	1-12
Institution of Holy Eucharist	3, 57
Internal Evidence, see Evidence.	
Irenæus, St.	21, 71, 72, 84

	PAGE
Irish Missionaries	90
Itacism	89
Jerome, St.	21, 53 note 1, 55, 75, 87, 98-9
Joanes	28
Julius Africanus	85
Justin Martyr	71, 84, 111
—— Ps.	85
Kilian, St.	90
Koum	28
Kuenen	35
Lachmann,	20-1, 22, 26, 32, 35, 38
Laurence, abp.	9

Lectionaries, value of, 102-3, 110-12 — their great virtual antiquity, 110, 117—a cause of error . . 109, 61, 101, 117

Lections	67
Lee, abp.	9
Leo the Great, St.	87
Leontius	85
Liturgies	110-12, 100 note 2, 117
Lombard Scribes	90

Lord's Prayer, the, 2—doxology in . . . 131-3, 100, 112

Lucian	79, 81, 98 note 4
Lucifer	85

Luke, St., why he wrote his gospel . . . . . 68 note

Macarius Magnes	85

Manuscripts, 87-90 — relative value of, 93, 117. Also 6, 7, 17. See Codex.

Marcion	70, 85

	PAGE
Mark, St., 78—why he wrote his gospel, 68 note — last twelve verses . 125-7, 1, 33, 96, 111	
Marsh, bp.	16
Martin, Abbè	36
Matthæi, C. F., 16-17, 107— his accuracy 16, 31	
Matthew, St., why he wrote his gospel	68 note
Melitene	28, 121
Michelsen, Dr.	36
Mill, Dr. John . . 13-14, 17, 31	
Moldenhawer	17
Monasteries	89
Monte Cassino	89
Nazara	28
Neutral Text (so-called) . 41, 51	
New Testament, passages quoted from—	
St. Matt. i. 25	57
,, iv. 13	28
,, — 23	27
,, v. 22	57
,, — 44	57
,, vi. 4	57
,, — 13 . . 2, 112, 131 &c.	
,, — 18	57
,, viii. 5	58
,, x. 25	28
,, xi. 16 . . 57, 121	
,, — 23	58
,, xii. 47	57
,, xiv. 6	27
,, — 29	58
,, xv. 13	58
,, — 22	28

	PAGE
New Testament, passages quoted from—(*continued*).	
St. Matt. xv. 32	58
,, — 39	58
,, xvi. 2, 3	57
,, — 12	58
,, xvii. 21	28
,, — 22	58
,, — 23	58
,, xviii. 11	57
,, xx. 16	57
,, — 22	57
,, — 23	57
,, xxi. 19	58
,, — 31	122
,, xxiii. 14	57
,, xxvi. 28	57
,, — 39	112
,, xxvii. 33	57
,, — 49	3
,, xxviii. 9	57
,, — 19	58
St. Mark i. 39	27
,, ii. 5	58
,, — 9	58
,, iii. 28	58
,, — 29	58
,, v. 41	28
,, vi. 11	57
,, — 21	59
,, — 22	27
,, — 33 . . 42, 57	
,, — 36	57
,, vii. 3	58
,, — 16	57
,, viii. 26	57
,, ix. 29	57
,, — 44	57
,, — 46	57

INDEX

New Testament, passages quoted from—(*continued*).	PAGE	New Testament, passages quoted from—(*continued*).	PAGE
St. Mark x. 6	57	St. Luke xiv. 44	57
,, — 7	57	,, xvi. 12	58
,, — 21	57	,, xvii. 6	59
,, — 24	57	,, — 19	57
,, xi. 8	57	,, — 36	57
,, — 19	59	,, — 24	57
,, — 22	59	,, xxii. 19, 20	2, 27
,, — 26	57	,, — 43, 44	2, 53, 111, 128 &c.
,, xii. 30	57		
,, — 33	57	,, — 55	58
, xiii. 14	59	,, — 64	57
,, — 18	57	,, xxiii. 17	57
,, xiv. 22-24	57	,, — 34	2, 53, 111, 127 &c.
,, — 35	59		
,, — 68	57	,, — 38	3
,, xv. 39	3	,, — 45	2
,, xvi. 4	58	,, xxiv. 1	57
,, — 9-20	1, 53, 96, 123 &c.	,, — 3	27
		,, — 6	27
St. Luke i. 28	57	,, — 9	27
,, ii. 14	53, 58, 96, 125 &c.	,, — 12	3, 27
		,, — 15	2
,, iv. 4	57	,, — 36	3, 27
,, — 5	57	,, — 40	3, 27
,, — 16	28	,, — 42	57
,, — 44	27	,, — 52	27
,, vi. 1	57, 120	,, — 53	57
,, — 26	57	St. John i. 27	57
,, — 45	57	,, iii. 13	57, 133 &c.
,, viii. 16	57		
,, — 43	57	,, v. 3, 4	3, 57
,, ix. 55, 56	57	,, vi. 51	57
,, x. 22	57	,, vii. 53 — viii. 11	121
,, — 42	58		
,, xi. 2-4	2	,, viii. 59	57
,, xii. 56	58, 120	,, xiii. 32	57
,, xiv. 10	59	,, xiv. 1	112

INDEX.

New Testament, passages quoted from—(*continued*).	PAGE	New Testament, passages quoted from—(*continued*).	PAGE
St. John xiv. 4	57	Heb. vii. 21	57
,, xvi. 16	57	James i. 20	58
,, xix. 17	28	1 Pet. iii. 1	59
Acts iii. 6	57	2 Pet. ii. 12	58
,, x. 19	27	1 John v. 7	9
,, — 30	57	Nicæa, Council of	14, 52
,, xi. 11	28	Nisibis	51
,, xii. 25	28		
,, xiii. 7	59	Oral teaching	67
,, xv. 18	57	Origen . 18, 21, 22, 71, 78-80, 85	
,, — 24	57	Origenism	78 &c.
,, xvi. 13	59	Orthodox, no evidence that they depraved Holy Scripture	69, 121 note 5
,, xviii. 7	28		
,, — 21	57		
,, xxi. 22	57		
,, — 25	57	Pamphilus, 79, 80, 81, 83— library of	91
,, xxiv. 6, 7, 8	57	Pantænus	78
,, xxv. 13	58	Patristic Era	86 &c., 104
,, xxvii. 13	58	Paragraphs, bible, due to Bengel	16
,, xxviii. 1	28, 121		
,, — 29	57	Paul, St., Pauline Epistles 101—number of MSS. of,	106, 107
Rom. v. 1	58		
,, — —	59	Peace be unto you	3
,, xv. 24	57	Pericope adulteræ	121
1 Cor. iii. 1	58	Peter of Alexandria	41
,, ix. 24	3	Philo	77
,, xiii. 3	58	Philoxenus	103
,, — 5	29	Piercing of our Lord's Side	3, 96
2 Cor. v. 14	57	Pierius	80
Eph. i. 1	57	Polycarp, St., Martyrdom of	73
,, — 15	57	——— translator	103
Col. iii. 6	57	Praxapostoli	112
1 Thess. i. 1	57	Priscian	88
,, ii. 7	58	Ptolemy Euergetes	90
1 Tim. iii. 16	53, 134 &c.		
Tit. ii. 5	58		
Heb. ii. 7	57	Question, nature of the	64

Quotations from Ecclesiastical
Writers 116-7
Received Text, when first so-
called, 11—nature of, 12—
relation to Traditional Text,
12, 63, 119—rejected by
Lachmann, 21—by Tregel-
les, 22—how treated by Tischendorf, 25—by Westcott
and Hort, 27, 30—by Sound
Textualists 32, 33
Reiche, J. G. 17, 35
Revised Version, number of
changes in, 3 note—mainly
follows Westcott and Hort,
29-30. Also 26, 28, 34, 38 note
Roman Catholic opinion . . 36

Sanday, Professor, 38 note,
76 note 3, 114 note 3
Saracens 90, 91
Scholz 18
Scriptures, the Holy, corpo-
rate as well as individual
productions 67
Scrivener, Dr., his works and
opinions, 30-32, 11, 12
note, 18 and notes 2 and 3,
26 note 1, 46, 50, 52 note,
55, 56, 60, 61, 69 note 2,
82, 106, 107, 114
Semler 17
Serapeum 90
Severus 96
Sharpe, abp. 14
Simon Magus 70
Sinai, Mt. 25
SON of GOD, the, Eternal
Existence of 133-4

Sound Textualism . 30-37, 60-4
Stephen, Robert, his editions,
10, 11, 12, 14, 15
—— Henry 10, 11
Stunica 8, 9
Syrian Text—no foundation
for this term, 39 note, 51-54.
See Traditional Text.

Tatian, his diatessaron, 71,
80 note 6
Tatian, Ps. 85
Tertullian . . . 71, 72, 73, 84
Textual Criticism, prevailing
ignorance of, 4—history of 6-37
Textualism, Sacred, how dif-
fers from Classical . . . 65-8
Theodoret 71
Theodosius 90
Theophilus of Antioch . . . 84
Tischendorf, his great works
and labours, 23-25—not a
trustworthy judge of principles, 27 . . Also 55, 56, 82
Titius or Titus Justus . . 28, 121
Titus of Bostra 85
Traditional Text, not the same
as the Received Text, 12,
13, 63, 119—when settled,
91 &c.—the great object of
discovery, 119-20—the true
Text, 62-4—admitted by
Extreme Textualists to go
back to St. Chrysostom, 23
—called "Syrian" and
treated as worthless by
Westcott and Hort, 42-3—
—not a late invention, 51,

INDEX.

53-4—dates from the first, 73, 83-5. Also 51, 101, 102, 107

Transcribing, art of, 7, 88-90, 93, 102

Tregelles, S. P., his labours and books 21-3, 32

Uncial Manuscripts, 105-6—table of, 108-9—opposition of Cursives to, a figment, 102 . . . . Also 16, 22, 60

Uncouth names in B . . . 28

Vercellone 36, 56

Versions, 113-15—table of, 113 —older than manuscripts, 117—value of, 114-5. Also 6, 7, 22, 16, 34, 43, 61, 73, 102
    Anglo-Saxon 103
    Arabic 103
    Armenian 99
    Bahiric, see Memphitic.
    Bashmuric 98
    Curetonian Syriac, 51, 74 note, 100 note 2
    Elearchian, see Bashmuric.
    Ethiopian 99
    Frankish 103
    Georgian 99
    Gothic . . . 94-5, 13, 98
    Harclean 103
    Italic, see Old Latin.
    Latin, Old, 76 and note 3, 21, 85, 98, 115
    Memphitic . . 76-7, 13, 98

Versions—(*continued*).
    Persic 103
    Peshito, 74-5, 51, 85, 98, 100 note 2
    Philoxenian 103
    Sahidic, see Thebaic.
    Slavonic 103
    Thebaic, 76-7, 98, 100 note 2
    Vulgate 98-99

Victor of Antioch 96
Vincentius 85

Wake, abp. 14
Walker, John 15
Walton, bp. 13
Westcott, Professor, 25-30, 38-59, 35
Western Readings . . . 41, 51
Wetstein 16, 96
Woide 15
Word, the first from the Cross 127-8, 2
Wordsworth, Bp. Christopher 35 and note 2, 77
—— Bp. Charles 35
—— Bp. John . . . 76 note 3
Worship, Common 68
Written records, scarcity of at first 71

Xenaias 103
Ximenes, cardinal 7-9

Youth of Textual Science . 20-30

Zacynthius, see Codex.
Zeno, emperor 97

Order Blank (p. 1)

Name:_____

Address:_____

City & State:_____Zip:_____

Credit Card #:_____Expires:_____
- [ ] Send *Guide to N.T. Textual Criticism* by Edward Miller ($11 +$4) A new hardback reprint, 168 pages
- [ ] Send *The Last 12 Verses of Mark* by Dean Burgon ($15+$4 S&H) A hardback book 400 pages.
- [ ] Send *The Revision Revised* by Dean Burgon ($25 + $4 S&H) A hardback book, 640 pages in length.
- [ ] Send *The Traditional Text* hardback by Burgon ($16 + $4 S&H) A hardback book, 384 pages in length.
- [ ] Send *Causes of Corruption* by Burgon ($15 + $4 S&H) A hardback book, 360 pages in length.
- [ ] Send *Inspiration and Interpretation*, Dean Burgon ($25+$4 S&H) A hardback book, 610 pages in length.
- [ ] Send *Vindicating Mark 16:9-20* by Dr. Waite ($3+$3 S&H)
- [ ] Send *Westcott & Hort's Greek Text & Theory Refuted by Burgon's Revision Revised--Summarized* by Dr. D. A. Waite ($7.00 + $3 S&H), 120 pages, perfect bound.
- [ ] Send *Summary of Traditional Text* by Dr. Waite ($3 +$2)
- [ ] Send *Summary of Causes of Corruption*, DAW ($3+$2)
- [ ] Send *Summary of Inspiration* by Dr. Waite ($3 + $2 S&H)
- [ ] Send *Burgon's Warnings on Revision* by DAW ($7+$3 S&H) A perfect bound book, 120 pages in length.
- [ ] Send *Fundamentalist MIS-INFORMATION on Bible Versions* by Dr. Waite ($7+$3 S&H) perfect bound, 136 pages
- [ ] Send *Holes in the Holman Christian Standard Bible* by Dr. Waite ($3+$2 S&H) A printed booklet, 40 pages
- [ ] Send *Central Seminary Refuted on Bible Versions* by Dr. Waite ($10+$3 S&H) A perfect bound book, 184 pages
- [ ] Send *Fundamentalist Distortions on Bible Versions* by Dr. Waite ($6+$3 S&H) A perfect bound book, 80 pages

Send or Call Orders to:
THE BIBLE FOR TODAY
900 Park Ave., Collingswood, NJ 08108
Phone: 856-854-4452; FAX:--2464; Orders: 1-800 JOHN 10:9
E-Mail Orders: BFT@BibleForToday.org; Credit Cards O K

Order Blank (p. 2)

Name:_____

Address:_____

City & State:_____Zip:_____

Credit Card #:_____Expires:_____

Other Materials on the KJB & T.R.

[ ] Send *The Case for the King James Bible* by DAW ($7 +$3 S&H) A perfect bound book, 112 pages in length.
[ ] Send *Foes of the King James Bible Refuted* by DAW ($10 +$4 S&H) A perfect bound book, 164 pages in length.
[ ] Send *Contemporary Eng. Version Exposed*, DAW ($3+$2)
[ ] Send *Defending the King James Bible* by Dr. Waite $13 | $4 S&H) A hardback book, indexed with study questions.
[ ] Send *Westcott's Denial of Resurrection*, Dr. Waite ($4+$3)
[ ] Send *Four Reasons for Defending KJB* by DAW ($3+$3)
[ ] Send *Dean Burgon's Confidence in KJB* by DAW ($3+$3)
[ ] Send *Readability of A.V. (KJB)* by D. A. Waite, Jr. ($6 +$3)
[ ] Send *NIV Inclusive Language Exposed* by DAW ($5+$3)
[ ] Send *26 Hours of KJB Seminar* (4 videos) by DAW ($50.00)
[ ] Send *Heresies of Westcott & Hort* by Dr. Waite ($7+$3)
[ ] Send *Scrivener's Greek New Testament Underlying the King James Bible*, hardback, $14+$4 S&H
[ ] Send *Scrivener's Annotated Greek New Testament*, by Dr. Frederick Scrivener: Hardback--$35+$5 S&H; Genuine Leather--$45+$5 S&H
[ ] Send *Why Not the King James Bible?--An Answer to James White's KJVO Book* by Dr. K. D. DiVietro, $10+$4 S&H
[ ] Send *Forever Settled--Bible Documents & History Survey* by Dr. Jack Moorman, $20+$4 S&H. Hardback book.
[ ] Send *Early Church Fathers & the A.V.--A Demonstration* by Dr. Jack Moorman, $6 + $4 S&H.
[ ] Send *When the KJB Departs from the So-Called "Majority Text"* by Dr. Jack Moorman, $16 + $4 S&H

Send or Call Orders to:
THE BIBLE FOR TODAY
900 Park Ave., Collingswood, NJ 08108
Phone: 856-854-4452; FAX:--2464; Orders: 1-800 JOHN 10:9
E-Mail Orders: BFT@BibleForToday.org; Credit Cards OK

Order Blank (p. 3)

Name:_____

Address:_____

City & State:_____Zip:_____

Credit Card#:_____Expires:_____

More Materials on the KJB &T.R.

[ ] Send #2987 *Bob Jones University's Inconsistent Position on the Textus Receptus & the T.R.* @ $2.00 + $1.00 S&H

[ ] Send *Dean Burgon Society Meetings* (2000) in Elkton, MD
Audios--#2999/1-9 @ $27.00 + $4.00 S&H
Videos--#2999VC1-2 @ $25.00 + $5.00 S&H
Message Book: #2999-P, 156 pages @ $15.00+$4.00 S&H

[ ] Send *Dean Burgon Society Meetings* (2001) in Ramsey,MN
Audios--#3037/1-9 @ $27.00 + $4.00 S&H
Videos--#3037VC1-2 @ $25.00 + $5.00 S&H
Message Book: #3037-P, 124 pages @ $12.00+$4.00 S&H

[ ] Send *Dean Burgon Society Meetings* (2002) in Arden, NC
Audios--#3075/1-7 @ $21.00 + $4.00 S&H
Videos--#3075VC1-2 @ $25.00 + $5.00 S&H
Message Book: #3075-P, 172 pages @ $17.00+$4.00 S&H

[ ] Send *Missing in Modern Bibles--Nestle-Aland & NIV Errors* by Dr. Jack Moorman, $8 + $4 S&H

[ ] Send *The Doctrinal Heart of the Bible--Removed from Modern Versions* by Dr. Jack Moorman, VCR, $15 +$4 S&H

[ ] Send *Modern Bibles--The Dark Secret* by Dr. Jack Moorman, $5 + $2 S&H

[ ] Send *Early Manuscripts and the A.V.--A Closer* Look, by Dr. Jack Moorman, $15 + $4 S&H

[ ] Send the "DBS Articles of Faith & Organization" (N.C.)

[ ] Send Brochure #1: "1000 Titles Defending KJB/TR"(N.C.)

Send or Call Orders to:
THE BIBLE FOR TODAY
900 Park Ave., Collingswood, NJ 08108
Phone: 856-854-4452; FAX:--2464; Orders: 1-800 JOHN 10:9
E-Mail Orders: BFT@BibleForToday.org; Credit Cards OK

The Defined King James Bible

UNCOMMON WORDS DEFINED ACCURATELY

I. Deluxe Genuine Leather

✦Large Print--Black or Burgundy✦

1 for $40.00+$6 S&H

✦Case of 12 for✦

$30.00 each+$30 S&H

✦Medium Print--Black or Burgundy✦

1 for $35.00+$5 S&H

✦Case of 12 for✦

$25.00 each+$24 S&H

II. Deluxe Hardback Editions

1 for $20.00+$6 S&H (Large Print)

✦Case of 12 for✦

$15.00 each+$30 S&H (Large Print)

1 for $15.00+$5 S&H (Medium Print)

✦Case of 12 for✦

$10.00 each+$24 S&H (Medium Print)

Order Phone: 1-800-JOHN 10:9

CREDIT CARDS WELCOMED

www.ingramcontent.com/pod-product-compliance
Lightning Source LLC
Chambersburg PA
CBHW060537100426
42743CB00009B/1557